# MY CHEMICAL
# ROMANCE

## This Band
## Will Save
## Your Life

# MY CHEMICAL ROMANCE

## This Band Will Save Your Life

REINHARDT HAYDN

Plexus, London

FOR ABBEY DALLETT

All rights reserved including the right of
reproduction in whole or in part in any form
Copyright © 2008 by Plexus Publishing Limited
Published by Plexus Publishing Limited
25 Mallinson Road
London SW11 1BW
www.plexusbooks.com
First printing 2008

British Library Cataloguing in Publication Data

Haydn, Reinhardt
   My Chemical Romance : this band will save your life
   1. My Chemical Romance (Musical group)
   I. Title
   782.4'2166'0922

   ISBN-10: 0-85965-416-8
   ISBN-13: 978-0-85965-416-6

Cover photograph by Steve Brown/Retna
Cover design by Rebecca Longworth
Book design by Coco Wake-Porter
Printed in Great Britain by Scotprint, Glasgow.

# CONTENTS

# EVERYONE HERE GETS OUT ALIVE

**'If you keep believing in us, we'll never stop believing in you.'**
**– Gerard Way**

As rock phenomena go, My Chemical Romance are *different*. Sure, like a hundred other bands, the New Jersey quintet sell records, fill dance halls and appear on the covers of magazines worldwide. In addition to the uniqueness of their accessible, genre-transcending sound, what sets them apart is the very personal manner in which the group interact with their fans.

Although My Chemical Romance possess a sound and image that is theatrical, grandiose and eminently suited to spectacular performances in vast arenas, their lyrics and individual statements are shot through with an understanding of the private, often unspoken fears and difficulties that are common within the minefield of adolescence. The band, led by vocalist and songwriter Gerard Way, have made a point of bringing topics such as bullying, self-harm, isolation and teenage depression into the rock milieu – and, in doing so, have connected with an entire generation of young people whose thoughts and feelings made them feel like misfits and outcasts.

Unlike the many performers who have an agenda that includes changing the world, smashing the system, or saving the planet, the My Chem manifesto sees their fanbase as individuals rather than a vast demographic they can mobilise in order to make a

*My Chemical Romance: (L-R) Ray Toro (Guitar); Mikey Way (Bass);*
*Gerard Way (Vocals); Frank Iero (Bass); Bob Bryar (Drums).*

point or promote a specific cause. This group have a one-item programme: that their followers pass through the difficulties of growing up, intact and able to function. 'The main thing that we've always wanted to do was to save people's lives,' Gerard told *Alternative Press*. 'That sounds Mother Teresa-ish and outlandish, but it really does happen. It does make a huge difference. We've seen it in action.'

An exploration of the many MCR fan forums bear out Gerard's assertions, with scores of fans posting evocative accounts of the ways in which the band's lyrics and music have touched and helped them. Many of these teenagers find it difficult to open up to parents or other authority figures and have fallen through the cracks in established support networks. My Chemical Romance have provided an unconventional, but successful, source of inspiration and guidance to innumerable troubled fans who otherwise would have been isolated from any kind of practical assistance – possibly until it was too late.

As unfeasible as it may sound to cynics and outsiders, this band really *does* save lives. Kevin, a My Chem fan from Manchester, found that the group helped him to overcome the death of his aunt and the painful break-up of a relationship. 'I love what My Chemical Romance stand for, it's true and honest,' he wrote on *theblackparade.net* forum. 'They're my escape, my inspiration and my saviour.'

Many of those contributing their experiences to the forums have indulged in self-harm, or even attempted suicide as a means of striking back at a world which apparently has little time for them. Panita, from France, is one of those who assert that the group have helped her back from the brink of oblivion. 'Every time I feel like everything's all fucked up and I just want it all to end . . . there's Gerard's voice, echoing in my head, telling me that it's alright to be messed up, because you realise that everybody else is messed up . . . and then you overcome it.' Similarly, Susana from Los Angeles explained that discovering the band also meant discovering a group of real people that understood how she felt because they had experienced similar feelings. 'When I listened to their music I felt like these guys understood and cared. Because at that point I thought no one cared and I felt so alone that I would cry myself to sleep at night, hugging myself. As I got to know the band more, I realised they were just like me. They went through what I went through. I stopped drinking and haven't touched a drink since. I've stopped cutting for the most part, but old habits die hard.'

Perhaps more than anything, it is the common experience of feeling unloved, marginalised and desperate that has served to forge a unique bond between band and audience. As Gerard explained to *Metal Hammer* in 2006, My Chemical Romance was conceived as a collective front against hostility and indifference. 'We were originally united as a group because we ourselves were obvious outsiders. We were pretty much invisible and insignificant. When nobody pays any attention to you, you realise how mortal you are. That's why teenagers that are troubled or are seen as outcasts are drawn to death. You have a lot of time to examine that subject when you're all alone.'

From their earliest days, it became apparent to the quintet that being in MCR was providing them with a focus and direction they would otherwise have lacked. From that realisation, it required only a short leap of logic to see that the band could provide a clear demonstration of what can be achieved by 'misfits' and 'losers'.

'One thing we can say for sure is that the band saved our lives. I always thought we had something to offer,' observed guitarist Frank Iero, 'and I wanted to have some importance in my life, so this band was the best thing that ever happened to me. Before that I was on a fast track to doing nothing. I think we offer our fans a sanctuary rather than salvation. The band is a tool to save yourself. We're like a support group – the AA of saving lives.'

The intense belief that My Chemical Romance's hardcore following have in the band is reciprocated, and has created a mutually supportive dynamic; the group is empowered by the unprecedented levels of dedication shown them by their fans, while the fans are empowered by MCR's success and their openness about the kind of experiences that many of them have undergone, but would be uncomfortable discussing. 'I feel like we're definitely the champions for everybody who doesn't fit in,' observed Gerard in an interview with *Sugar* magazine. 'If you come to a MCR show, you're probably a little fucked up, and that's OK because we're just as fucked up as you. It's us against the world. And it's great because there's thousands of us in one place.'

The evidence that this message is not only striking a chord among the massed ranks of the MCRmy, but actually having genuine beneficial effects, can be found among the band's fan forums. Phoebe from London posted a statement summarising how the band's ethos had helped her overcome the death of her grandfather, depression and problems at school: 'Maybe I'm a bit fucked up, but that's okay, because I have the rest of MCR's fans that have gone through the same kinda shit as me. There's people out there that have it much worse, and now I can't thank MCR enough for saving my life. If it wasn't for them I wouldn't be here. If it wasn't for MCR I wouldn't be myself.'

For his part, Gerard is quick to assert that the fans' role in this mutually supportive dynamic is every bit as crucial as that of the band. 'It's all because of the fans,' he told *Big Cheese* in 2005. 'We've always been the underdogs and often our fans are underdogs with us. We're taking over the world with them. That's what's special. I've always said that if you don't believe in yourself, then people don't believe in you. Without that faith you have no power – you have nothing.'

In essence, the philosophy espoused by My Chemical Romance is simple and accessible – they encourage their fans to be themselves, accept others, and promote the idea of discussing problems and fears openly. Speaking to *Crush Media Magazine*'s Jason Schleweis and Rob Todd in 2004, Gerard was keen to stress the value of openness. 'We have been dealing with mental depression all our lives, and I mean everyone gets depressed but so few people address depression in music. And that's always just been one of our messages because so few people address what's wrong with them and communicate their problems.'

'The other message is like just fuckin' be who you want to be, be yourself, and live out everything you absolutely want to live,' Gerard told the *Punknews* website. 'We're up there, and we are like five, probably most self-conscious dudes in the world, and we get up there and we try to act like Queen . . . It's not very characteristic for people who have self esteem issues, you know.'

The importance to their fanbase of the transparent manner in which My Chem present their own insecurities cannot be underestimated – as Kelly, a Canadian site moderator on *theblackparade.net* forum recounted, 'I looked at them thinking "wow," they made it through – if they can do it, I can . . . today I am so different than I was a few years ago. That insecurity will always lie somewhere deep inside of me, and that's where their music still helps me today to laugh it off and carry on.'

Speaking to *Metal Hammer* in January 2006, Gerard offered his take on why the MCR manifesto has had a quantifiably positive effect on the band's fanbase: 'I think that what we offer is an alternative . . . people see a different way when they look at us. We're outsiders. We're the kids who didn't get dates for the prom. We're the kids who were confused, who didn't fit in with the cliques, who weren't part of the in-crowd. Growing up can be a very frightening and confusing time, and I think people look at us and see that it's okay to be different.'

Given their first-hand experience of being excluded, ignored and undermined, My Chemical Romance's attitude of inclusiveness is logical and commendable. Their aim is simply to rock without necessarily being 'rockist'. 'People definitely miss the Mötley Crüe antics, but that's not what we're about, because of the negative elements that go with it – mainly homophobia, racism and sexism,' Gerard explained. 'Punk rock and grunge made a difference, but nu-metal set things back again because it was all, "Let's

*MCR's unique relationship with their fans is made plain by the Brixton crowd in November 2006.*

beat the shit out of each other, get girls to show us their tits and fuck groupies." So yet again, we're trying to reverse that.'

'We like to be different from other hardcore bands by riding the line between homosexuality and heterosexuality just to push buttons and raise awareness,' Gerard declared. 'And one of the greatest things about our shows when you look out there is that you find a lot of kids that don't match each other at all. It's not like a scene show and that's the way we love it.'

Gerard avoids connecting the band to any kind of rigidly defined 'scene' and the group have sought to distance themselves from the nebulous 'emo' tag. 'Our music is, and always has been, intelligent,' he told the *Playmusic* website. 'Someone asked me the other day which side I was on in the emo war, and I just said "the other side". I mean, we're not emo, but there's nothing worth fighting about here, it's negative, it drags everyone down.'

'We like to just describe ourselves as a rock band, everything about us is just a rock band. If what people have to do is to put us into a category, that's fine you know, but if you think of a traditional emo band, that's not what this band's about,' drummer Bob Bryar told the *New Zealand Herald*. 'Our music is violent pop,' insisted Frank Iero. 'It's music to save your life.'

Although My Chem would not exist without their music, it's merely one aspect of what makes the group such a vital and relevant phenomenon. 'I think our attitude really sets us apart as far as why we're in this and what we do this for. It's not simply for the fun of being in a band or playing music, it really has nothing to do with that, or fame or money or anything,' Gerard told *thepunksite*'s Gary Hampton. 'We're in it because we love helping people and we really wanna be there for people and that's kind of, that's our attitude towards this band.'

On signing to Warner subsidiary label Reprise in 2003, MCR countered criticism that they had in some way 'sold out' by issuing a press statement that reaffirmed their core values: 'We started this band for ourselves, to bear our souls, purge our own personal demons, and reclaim our innocence. When you are told you are not good enough your entire life sometimes the only thing you can do is scream "fuck you" at the top of your lungs. This band was started and will end with three virtues: Honesty, Sincerity, and Loyalty.'

Since then, My Chem have remained steadfastly true to their word, and earned the loyalty and respect of fans such as Deborah from Western Australia, who wrote of the band's 2006 album, *The Black Parade*: 'This album got me through some really tough times in my life . . . I'm so thankful to these guys 'cause without them I know I wouldn't be here today. You got me to realise so many things, so thank you so much.'

'That's one of our goals – to help people get through really rough things,' insisted Bob Bryar. 'If anybody, even one person, will listen to us and go get help for anything they're thinking of doing by harming themselves, then we achieved our goal.'

In an age where much of popular culture is hardwired for mass consumption, My Chemical Romance's emphasis on the specific problems facing individuals is both welcome and admirable. 'We're a victory for the little people,' Gerard declared. 'Yes, we have success now and we have a great quality of life, we have a CD with our name on it and we have videos and all that stuff. But we're outcasts. There was a time when all we had was each other. People might like us, but what they see in us is themselves.'

As they have regularly acknowledged, the success that MCR have enjoyed in the past five years has been as much due to the support received from their fans as the creative talents of Gerard, Mikey, Frank, Ray and Bob. It is therefore fitting that as well as giving the band a focus and purpose, this success has also benefited their fans. 'They're not fucking ashamed of who they are any more,' Frank told *Guardian* music journalist Alexis Petridis. 'Because this cool band came out that is fucking retarded and ashamed and awkward like me, so maybe being retarded and ashamed and awkward is not a bad thing.'

'It's about making a difference,' explained Gerard. 'It's about giving those kids a representative.'

# Chapter 1

# SECRET ORIGINS

**'I love Jersey: There's pretty parts too. We just don't live in them.'
– Gerard Way**

Although one of the smaller American states, New Jersey is still a pretty sizeable territory that covers almost 9000 square miles and provides homes for nearly nine million people. Known as 'the Garden State', the area is characterised by a striking degree of social diversity, boasting the fourth highest *per capita* income in the country, while two of America's most economically deprived towns – Camden and Newark – are also to be found within its borders. Similarly, whereas almost half of the state is covered in woodland, New Jersey can also lay claim to over 100 toxic waste dumps.

Tucked away in the north-eastern corner of Essex County lies Belleville – birthplace of Gerard and Mikey Way. It's at the run-down end of the New Jersey scale; a blue-collar, predominantly Italian-American town sandwiched between the regional homicide capital of Newark and the petrochemical ugliness of Jersey City. Although the municipality has bestowed upon itself the nickname 'the Cherry Blossom Capital of America', it is better known for showing up in episodes of *The Sopranos* than for any agricultural distinction.

During the 1970s, Belleville's population shrank by around 6 per cent as those with sufficient incomes moved to more upmarket suburbs, while arriving migrants tended to settle in more urban districts. On Saturday 9 April 1977, this trend was very slightly

*MCR Mark I – with original drummer Matt 'Otter' Pelissier second right.*

reversed when Donald and Donna Way celebrated the birth of their first son, Gerard Arthur. The Ways were an unremarkable couple; Donald was employed as a service manager at an automobile dealership and Donna worked locally as a hairdresser. The family lineage was composed of a mixture of Italian and Scottish heritages, and the young family shared their modest home with Donna's parents, who doted on the new arrival.

A few months after Gerard's third birthday, the compact Way abode became a little more crowded thanks to the arrival of another baby boy. Born on Wednesday 10 September 1980, Michael James Way immediately looked up to his big brother, attempting to run like Gerard did before he could even walk – with the inevitable, often painful consequences.

> 'We all have very humble backgrounds and very geeky interests.' – Mikey Way

In addition to being America's ground zero for car thefts, the run-down areas of New Jersey play host to a whole range of criminality. 'There's a lot of shootings, drug related crimes, murders, things like that – Mafia related crimes,' explained Gerard. 'Our parents were kind of scared to let us outside of the house,' Mikey told *Alternative Press* journalist Scott Heisel, 'because where we lived was pretty dangerous.'

Ensconced in the safety zone of their home, the Way brothers formed a close understanding and exercised their highly active imaginations to construct their own fantasy worlds. 'What I had to do – and my brother had to do – was really create our own space in our heads,' recalled Gerard. 'I drew pictures, I made stories up, I lied a lot – I lived in my head.'

Although it was hardly ideal for two young boys to be shut indoors for the majority of their free time, this confinement served to ignite their creativity at an early age. Their maternal grandmother, ceramic artist Elena Lee Rush, was quick to notice Gerard and Mikey's creative potential, and encouraged the boys at every opportunity. 'My grandmother was a woman who inspired me and pushed Mikey and I towards those things,' Gerard told indie rock magazine *Wonkavision*. 'She knew we had this ability and so she pushed us towards it. She made us sing if she thought we could, learn how to act . . . she taught us how to use our imagination.'

In addition to Elena's patient encouragement, the brothers also benefited from the love and support of their parents. 'My dad shaped me morally,' revealed Gerard. 'My dad's a real man – a working class guy who worked hard for every single penny.'

'He's an amazing man who worked all his life, even weekends, so he could look after my brother and I,' Gerard told *NME*'s Imran Ahmed in 2006. 'From when I was a kid my dad said to me, "You can be whatever you want," and he was dead serious. He kept saying it 'til I was in my teens and I was like, "I got it," but not 'til I was 25.' In addition to providing his sons with values and guidance, by taking Gerard to a parade as a small boy, Donald Way also planted a seed that would germinate as *The Black Parade* some twenty years later.

By the time Gerard was in the third grade, he had begun to assemble a palette of interests that would furnish both him and Mikey with inspiration in later life. Both his mother and grandmother encouraged his growing interest in music – Elena bought Gerard his first guitar when he was eight years old, and around the same time Donna took him to his first concert. Appropriately enough for a Jersey boy, it was a Springsteen gig – 'The Boss' being his mother's favourite performer.

> **'Me and Mikey couldn't really play where we grew up, which was pretty much the same story with everybody, because it was so fucking dangerous.' – Gerard Way**

In addition to providing Gerard with an introduction to live rock'n'roll, Donna Way also shared her passion for the macabre with her sons. 'She would rent all these horror movies when we were really young and make us watch them with her,' Gerard told *Revolver* magazine. 'She loved anything with dolls or puppets that came alive,' added Mikey. 'I was terrified of the dark, and she had this porcelain doll collection that was really fucking creepy. I tried to get her to lock them up in a cupboard, but she never would.' 'She had hundreds of creepy dolls that she'd collected and there was a room in my house filled with nothing but creepy fucking dolls,' Gerard elaborated in a 2004 interview with *Kerrang!* 'I would have to walk through this room to get to my room and at night I'd hold my breath and run through the room because I was so terrified at the dolls.'

Gerard and Mikey were far more enthusiastic about the horror movies than Donna's dolls, and, despite the odd nightmare, the brothers developed a passion for such visceral visual fare that would stay with them all their lives. Along with comic books and rock music, horror films comprised the young Ways' main interests. It was hardly surprising that, almost as soon as they were old enough to go out and buy records, they gravitated towards bands that referenced elements of comic-book horror within their performances.

'Growing up, me and Gerard had always traded tunes of bands that we'd both been really into,' recalled Mikey. 'Me and him were both obsessed with Iron Maiden.' In addition to the east London band's raw approach to heavy metal, Gerard was enraptured by Maiden's showmanship and their iconic, cadaverous mascot, Eddie. 'I could pinpoint the live album by Iron Maiden, *Live After Death*, as the catalyst for me wanting to play music. From the theatrical intro to the thundering choruses – what else could you want in rock and roll? I was sold.' Gerard drew particular inspiration from Maiden vocalist Bruce Dickinson's command of the stage. 'He really inspired me 'cause he's a great frontman, a great singer and I've always been influenced by the way he sang.'

Even at this early stage, it was evident that Gerard was attracted to the kind of melodramatically enhanced rock that, twenty years later, would inform elements of My Chemical Romance's sound and image. In a 2007 interview with *Outburn* magazine, he cited Queen's lavish 1975 album *A Night At The Opera* as a significant influence on *The Black Parade*. 'I think Queen is the greatest rock band of all time . . . It was a collection of rock albums from the late '70s that had really impacted our childhoods and then later in our early twenties. We had that period where every one of us was obviously very much into punk rock, but before that, we were all listening to very classic rock albums as children.'

Ensconced in their bedroom, Gerard and Mikey continued developing their own shared universe filled with heavy metal, superheroes and celluloid horror. The creation of this private world represented a disengagement from the mundane elements of school and home life, and meant that the brothers were often quiet and withdrawn in public. 'I was a shy kid, so I lived in my head

> '[New Jersey]'s like New York's retarded brother, you know? That they keep locked up in the basement.' – Frank Iero

a lot,' Mikey told *Rock Sound*. 'The teachers thought there was something wrong with me because I wouldn't talk to other kids. I was almost playing mind games with them.'

Perhaps because neither Gerard nor Mikey readily befriended other children, their fraternal bond grew particularly strong. 'We didn't have anyone else to hang out with. We had friends from the neighbourhood, but it was mostly me and Gerard,' explained Mikey. 'We never fought,' Gerard recalled. 'We were inseparable. We hung out with each other constantly and still do. Every day, me and him stick together all day long.' Speaking to *Metal Hammer* in 2005, Ray Toro highlighted the brothers' closeness throughout their lives. 'I don't really picture them as brothers. They're more like best friends. I've never seen two brothers have a relationship like them.'

The affection shown him by his brother, parents and grandparents insulated Gerard from a world he described as 'way too tough for me when I was a little kid.' However, Gerard's sensitivity was such that he developed a mortal fear of losing his loved ones. 'When I was a kid, I was terrified of death,' he revealed to *Kerrang!* 'I used to wake up in the middle of the night having nightmares about my family and I'd be freaking out so they'd have to calm me down. It took me a good five years to get over that. I was afraid to go to school because I thought I would lose somebody. I don't know where that fear came from. I guess I was just overly sensitive.' Gerard's nightmares were so extreme that for a time he took to hiding bottles of cough syrup under his bed in order to sedate himself.

> **'We had to construct our own world we lived in constantly.' – Gerard Way**

In addition to his sometimes crippling sensitivity, Gerard experienced problems with his weight that increased the already considerable distance between himself and any kind of social life. 'I used to be fat,' he told the *NME*. 'I found out when I first lost a lot of weight that I could move really fast – I didn't get tired. Stairs weren't a problem. That's the ultimate outsider – the fat kid. You got a lot of things going against you: girls aren't interested in you, you don't fit in and you're always easy to make fun of.'

A further barrier to Gerard connecting with his peers manifested when he reached the fourth grade, and was moved to a new school as a means of giving the troubled youngster a fresh start. Although being the new kid in class is often a daunting and miserable experience, Gerard attempted to approach his situation with a positive outlook. 'It was really weird and so I thought maybe I'll try things; like I drew a lot more, I got involved in art programs and stuff. There was this drama club they had and I said, "Well, let me just try this."'

Encouraged by his grandmother and his drama teacher, the usually reticent Gerard tried out for a part and – to his astonishment – secured the lead role. 'I don't know how cool this is that I got the part, but I just kind of opened my mouth and was able to sing. And then my grandma was really excited about it. I wasn't so excited about it – I guess I just wanted to prove to myself that I could do it. Then after I got the part, I was stuck into doing it . . . She [grandma] made me this outfit and it was green tights, everything . . . Of course, it's a *great* idea to play Peter Pan your first year at a new school.'

After his success as the boy who never grew up, Gerard's vocal talent was recognised by his drama teacher, who called on him to sing whenever a suitable school function came around. 'He was kind of a shy kid when he was really young and he had all of these talents he was afraid to dwell on 'cos he was afraid he was gonna get made fun of, or he was afraid he wasn't good enough at them,' explained Mikey. 'One of these abilities was singing and at a young age he started to explore this voice that he had.'

Two years later, Gerard moved up into middle school, where he found he was marginalised by the tendency of his classmates to form cliques. 'Middle school's kind of the point where you're like, "Wait a minute – I used to hang out with all these kids and we used to be friends and that and now it's all about popularity,"' he recalled.

Rather than attempt to compete in a youthful scramble for status, Gerard curtailed his interest in drama and singing and returned to his and Mikey's private universe. 'I was like, "Why do I want to be this weird singer kid anymore?" I was into a lot of other stuff – I was into comic books and Iron Maiden and it

**'I wasn't bullied at school, I was just ignored.' – Gerard Way**

wasn't my thing so I kind of turned my back on it.'

Outside of school, Gerard spent much of his early adolescence discovering new music and playing *Dungeons & Dragons* – a clichéd pursuit of the ostracised and maladjusted. On Saturdays, his mother would drop him at a public library in Newark and he would spend the entire afternoon lost in studying the books. Aside from a short tenure working as a cart boy and bagger in a local grocery store, Gerard preferred to keep his interactions with the outside world to a minimum.

Chief among the groups that floated across Gerard's rapidly broadening horizon were horror-punks the Misfits, who hailed from Lodi, New Jersey – less than ten miles north of Belleville, near the end of Route 21. Specifically, it was the band's 1982 album *Walk Among Us* that ignited Gerard's passion for punk rock. 'This record changed everything for me,' he told *Guitar World* in 2005. 'My mom wouldn't buy it for me because it had a song called "Devil's Whorehouse", so I got my grandfather to buy it for me. I put it on and immediately I felt more liberated, free and pissed off than I'd ever been . . . I was an outcast and that record really got me through some bad times.'

Considered by many fans to be the Misfits' finest album, *Walk Among Us* combined the kind of catchy, riff-laden punk-metal epitomised by the Damned's 1979 disc, *Machine Gun Etiquette*, with the mix of horror and science fiction themes previously warped into a rock'n'roll format by psychobilly pioneers the Cramps. To top the whole zomboid formula off, frontman Glenn Danzig's lyrics dealt with a number of topics guaranteed to strike a chord with disenfranchised kids like Gerard – revenge upon school bul-

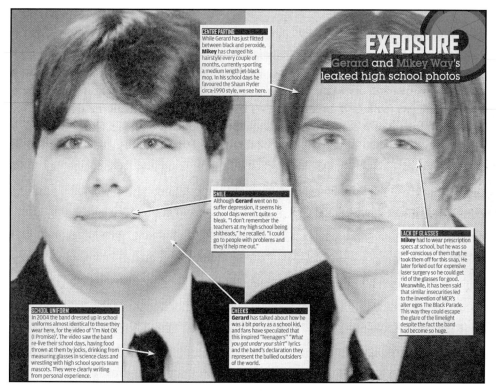

**EXPOSURE**
Gerard and Mikey Way's leaked high school photos

**CENTRE PARTING**
While Gerard has just flitted between black and peroxide, **Mikey** has changed his hairstyle every couple of months, currently sporting a medium length jet-black mop. In his school days he favoured the Shaun Ryder circa-1990 style, we see here.

**SMILE**
Although **Gerard** went on to suffer depression, it seems his school days weren't quite so bleak. "I don't remember the teachers at my high school being shitheads," he recalled. "I could go to people with problems and they'd help me out."

**LACK OF GLASSES**
**Mikey** had to wear prescription specs at school, but he was so self-conscious of them that he took them off for this snap. He later forked out for expensive laser surgery so he could get rid of the glasses for good. Meanwhile, it has been said that similar insecurities led to the invention of MCR's alter egos The Black Parade. This way they could escape the glare of the limelight despite the fact the band had become so huge.

**SCHOOL UNIFORM**
In 2004 the band dressed up in school uniforms almost identical to those they wear here, for the video of 'I'm Not OK (I Promise)'. The video saw the band re-live their school days, having food thrown at them by jocks, drinking from measuring glasses in science class and wrestling with high school sports team mascots. They were clearly writing from personal experience.

**CHEEKS**
**Gerard** has talked about how he was a bit porky as a school kid, and fans have speculated that this inspired "Teenagers" *"What you got under your shirt"* lyrics and the band's declaration they represent the bullied outsiders of the world.

*Gerard and Mikey's high school photos from Bellville High, with commentary from* NME.

lies ('Mommy, Can I Go Out And Kill Tonight'); visceral descriptions of the netherworld ('All Hell Breaks Loose'); and good ol' fashioned sinfulness ('Devil's Whorehouse').

As with Iron Maiden, the Misfits' lyrical explorations of horror, damnation and death keyed straight into Gerard's fascination with the macabre. 'I grew up as a kid obsessed with death. I was afraid of it, yet I couldn't look away from it,' he recalled. 'Being raised Catholic, you think you're going to hell. They straight up tell you as a child: "Everyone you know is going to die some day, and you don't know if you're

> **'No one likes the new kid in school. Because he smells weird and has a penchant for leather and the homoerotic.' – Gerard Way**

going to see them, because they might go to hell.'"

Like Peter Murphy, vocalist with iconic Goth outfit Bauhaus, Gerard found that his Catholic upbringing generated a fascination with the darker aspects of faith, and caused him to rebel against the overly straight and narrow path of righteousness. 'We were told that after we died we would definitely either go to Hell or Heaven. Hell seemed to be the more likely place, just because we did all the stuff they said was bad, like jerking off and cursing.'

By the time Gerard started at Belleville High School, he had become something close to the textbook loner. 'I was really quiet, I was very alone,' he recalled. 'I didn't connect with anyone at my high school whatsoever, and to this day, I still only talk to one person that I went to high school with. I think that happening causes you to have to use your imagination a lot and really just hang out with yourself.'

'On my first day in high school I sat all alone at lunchtime,' Gerard told Kerrang! 'It was the classic story – the weird kid in the army jacket, horror movie t-shirt and long, black hair. I was more interested in music and being creative. People were never really mean to me; they mostly just left me alone. I think really, I just wanted to be alone.'

> **'Jersey is full of vampires. They get together and play those role playing games, and then they think they're really vampires so they sit around and drink each others' blood.' – Gerard Way**

Isolated from his peers, Gerard gradually embraced the role of the outsider. 'I became very observant – a watcher. Very creepy I would say. I learned to see beauty in everything and ugliness in everything. I developed a very honest perspective.' At times this perspective manifested in a perverse manner. One such occasion was during an art class life-drawing session. 'There was this real beautiful model once, but she had a scar on her stomach and I made sure to pay a lot of attention to that. I thought that made her more attractive in a way.'

Throughout high school, Gerard continued to hone his drawing technique and was a regular at his local comic store, where he absorbed the various literary and visual talents of noted 1990s creators such as Grant Morrison, Richard Case and Todd McFarlane. 'I found solace in the comic book store,' he confessed. 'That saved my life.'

*Gerard, Mikey and Ray cut loose during one of My Chem's first New York showcase gigs in 2003.*

Although the complex, often surreal, post-*Watchmen* plots of Grant Morrison's run on DC's *Doom Patrol* comic would later influence the concepts behind *The Black Parade*, Gerard was also receptive to the more simplistic tales of retribution and triumph over adversity found in more mainstream titles. 'Growing up, I always wanted to be Batman, because he was just a normal dude,' he explained to *Spin* in 2005. 'Superman was all-perfect and had a duty to protect people. For Batman, it was a compulsion, like a religious thing. All the best heroes are ordinary people who make themselves extraordinary.'

Eventually, Gerard hung out at the comic store so often that he was offered a job there. While vastly superior to bagging groceries, this part-time gig came to a sudden and shocking end. 'I was working at the comic store, just watching animé, and we got held up,' he revealed to the *NME*. 'They put me on the ground and put a .357 Magnum to the back of my head, execution style. I lost a lot of innocence after that. The comic book store closed two weeks later.'

## 'I didn't become popular until senior year when punk rock started to become popular.' – Gerard Way

Although Gerard's detachment from his high school peers precluded opportunities to score with girls, puberty had worked its neurohormonal magic. 'I used to stalk [actress] Christina Ricci; she lived right here in Upper Montclair,' he confessed. 'Picture a fat kid – I plumped up pretty good, working at a comic store and eating cheeseburgers all the time – really far from my house and stranded in the middle of nowhere . . . I was really into this creepy little girl. This girl looks like an alien, but there's something really beautiful about her.'

When Gerard was fifteen, he again picked up the guitar that his grandmother had given him seven years earlier. However, his lack of interest in taking lessons undermined the possibility of a meteoric rise from weird obsessive loner to axe hero. 'I thought I was going to be in a rock band and play guitar. I wasn't very good. I joined this band I was really psyched on and I couldn't play "Sweet Home Alabama" on guitar and I got kicked out.'

This rejection only exacerbated Gerard's feelings of alienation and once more caused him to withdraw within himself. 'There was a moment in my life when I really wanted to kill myself. But even in my most jaded times, I had some hope,' he told US gossip magazine *Sugar*. 'I found my niche by becoming enchanted with these things . . .

things like ugliness, violence, tragedy,' he explained. 'I started to find humour in those things and find those things funny. Death became a huge joke to me and I had a very "fuck you" attitude towards death.'

Inspired by the noise and fury of hardcore punk trailblazers Black Flag's 1980 EP track 'Revenge', Gerard became obsessed with the concept of exacting vengeance on those who had harassed, ignored or mocked him. As he revealed on the *Life On The Murder Scene* DVD: 'I was obsessed with revenge because in high school I was such an outcast and I was always fantasising, and I had these revenge fantasies.'

However, Gerard's newly acquired nihilistic outlook received a massive jolt when he was sixteen. One of his small circle of friends committed suicide by throwing himself in front of an oncoming train. 'The suicide of my friend was something that really changed my life,' he explained in a 2006 *Metal Hammer* interview. 'There was a really strange wake where there were all these kids from high school there, all of his classmates – kids. That was strange. That set me on a path of wanting to escape that kind of life in New Jersey, the feeling of being depressed and insignificant.'

At the time, Gerard saw the possibility of breaking into comics or animation as the most likely means of escape from his increasingly oppressive surroundings. However, in 1995 he experienced another rock'n'roll epiphany, when Mikey paid for him to see the Smashing Pumpkins tour their newly released album, *Mellon Collie And The Infinite Sadness*, at Madison Square Garden. 'I was really into them, but I was more of a hermit,' he told *Rolling Stone*'s Austin Scaggs. 'Mikey was such a devout Pumpkins fan that he followed them up and down the East Coast. He had tickets to every gig.'

As Gerard recalled, his brother had hit upon an unconventional means of funding his concert going. 'Mikey was bootlegging Disney movies that were only out, like, in the Philippines – like *Song of the South* and *The Black Cauldron* – which he'd fucking sell on eBay. A private investigator came to our house, and he got nabbed. But they didn't throw him in jail. He was fifteen.'

Catching the full force of the Pumpkins' intense, multi-layered sound, and guitarist/vocalist Billy Corgan's unique delivery of his heartfelt, anguished lyrics, had a profound effect on the teenage brothers. 'It was the most inspirational thing I've ever seen,' Mikey recalled in a *Kerrang!* interview. 'As we sat there Gerard turned to me and said, "This is what we've got to do." I said, "I know, dude."'

# THE 21ST CENTURY WILL NOT NOW HAPPEN AS PLANNED

# Chapter 2

**'When we went to high school we were definitely the kids that didn't fit in. I used to wear a lot of black and get hassled for it.'**
**– Gerard Way**

I n 1995, Gerard graduated from Belleville High School and enrolled in a four-year fine arts degree course at the School of Visual Arts in Manhattan. Established in 1947, the college has well-established cartooning and animation departments, alongside those devoted to more conventional disciplines. Although his course emphasised a traditional artistic perspective, the fact that Spider-Man co-creator Steve Ditko and underground comics heavyweight Peter Bagge had attended the school indicated a path to the kind of career that Gerard had in mind.

Gerard's selection of a fine arts degree provided him with the kind of solid grounding in essential visual techniques that a significant number of contemporary comic book artists – whose styles often draw solely from the medium in which they work – often do not possess. 'The first year was a foundation year and it really, really taught me how to look at the world, in such a way that I still use the same skills that I developed,' he explained. 'I developed my senses a great deal. Talent can only take you so far; it's your own point of view on the world that makes a difference in art.'

For Gerard, it seemed possible that completing the course would enable him to escape the gravity well of mediocrity awaiting him back in Belleville. 'In Jersey, there's

*My Chem face the cameras for Fuse TV's* Daily Download *show, November 2004.*

a 99 per cent chance you're not going to do anything with your life,' he told *Blender's* Dorian Lynskey. 'Where we're from, a suburb of a city, there's nothing to do but drink, fight and fuck. It's very easy to get caught in this fucking working-class, punch-the-clock, get-bombed, and try-to-find-someone-to-poke lifestyle.'

In addition to providing him with a firm technical basis to his artistic technique, the less formalised environment of college also enabled Gerard to emerge from his self-imposed shell. 'I went to school in drag, in art school and my day was completely different because everybody thought I was a chick,' he told the *Trouble Bunch Music* site. 'I went as a girl, as like an experiment and it worked really well and everyone was really nice to me but I couldn't talk obviously . . . You know train conductors were really cool to me on my commute.'

> ## 'All of us grew up as geeks, getting picked on and being told we weren't good enough.' – Gerard Way

During the four years that Gerard was making his daily trips to and from Manhattan, a unique rock scene was developing on his home turf. Centring on a basement space occupied by Thursday frontman Geoff Rickly, a loose collection of local bands and their followers began gathering for regular shows. 'We just wanted to have a place for people in the area to come see music. It wasn't the most original idea, but I had a house in New Brunswick I was renting with a basement, and it just grew out of that,' Rickly told *New York Times* journalist Tammy La Gorce. 'It was a little sanctuary of a place. So many kids would show up that we'd open the storm windows so they could hear. One time we flagged down an ice cream truck for 300 kids.'

'Sometimes the parties were totally impromptu. It was just a bunch of guys at the house getting drunk, having fun, getting arrested and having to go to jail,' recalled Rickly in an interview with *Alternative Press*. 'Then there were these huge parties Alex [Saavedra, Eyeball Records' founder] would throw that would be a few hundred people at the house. Half the Jersey scene would be there. It would be everyone from the kids who'd go to the shows, to a lot of the bands, to everyone who ran the clubs.'

Established local bands such as the Bouncing Souls and Lifetime (who recorded the track 'Theme Song For A New Brunswick Basement Show' for their 1997 album *Jersey's Best Dancers*) began appearing at hastily convened events organised by Rickly and others, such as Alex Saavedra. Meanwhile, groups of fans and students from the nearby

Rutgers University organised their own gigs at local halls where the lack of a bar meant kids of all ages could get involved. 'Back when I was still going to clubs, I used to see a lot of bands in this place called the Pipeline in Newark,' Gerard told *Guitar World's* Richard Bienstock. 'But it wasn't a great environment for kids like me and my brother. There was always a lot of drunken idiots there and people getting into fights and knifing each other. It was really dangerous.'

Many of these local halls were owned by non-profit organisations such as the Veterans of Foreign Wars, the American Legion and the Elks, and a network of such venues became established in New Jersey towns such as Boonton, Wayne, Lyndhurst and Manville. The popularity of these home-grown shows mushroomed and soon began attracting out-of-state bands. 'You had all these suburban kids who weren't bothering to go out to the clubs in the city, and as a result all these touring bands started coming to them,' explained Gabe Saporta, former vocalist with New Brunswick alternative rock quartet Midtown. 'I remember us and Saves The Day did a show at the Manville (Elks Lodge) with the Get Up Kids and New Found Glory. At the Drive-In played there too, and Jimmy Eat World packed the Wayne Firehouse.'

Gerard and Mikey regularly attended these shows, and began making connections with some of the scene's more prominent personalities. Perhaps surprisingly, it was the younger

> **'I'm the kind of person that if I don't have a purpose, I'm dead.' – Gerard Way**

Way who proved to be a gregarious presence amidst the interlocking social circles of gigs and house parties. 'Mikey was always the more sociable one who'd come out to the parties that we threw,' Geoff Rickly told *Kerrang!* 'He could be really crazy. He'd stay over at our house and we'd often have to ask him, "Who the hell was that girl with you last night?" He'd say, "I've no idea." He was a little out of control.'

Whereas Gerard was committed to breaking into comic books or cartooning, his younger brother was primarily orientated towards rock'n'roll. After leaving high school in 1998, Mikey had half-heartedly enrolled in further education with a view to putting a band together. 'I thought college was a place you went to find people to be in a band with,' he told *Blender* in 2005.

Mikey's connection to the burgeoning local rock scene was consolidated when he scored an internship at Eyeball Records. The Kearny-based label had been founded in 1995 by Alex Saavedra, and was forging a reputation for discovering new talent and promoting new local bands such as Midtown and Geoff Rickly's Thursday, alongside established hardcore groups like Breakdown and the Casualties. In addition to putting up flyers and helping out around the office, Mikey established a good relationship with Saavedra and became a fixture at Eyeball's concerts and parties.

More often than not, Gerard would prefer to stay home and hone his drawing skills. On the occasions he did venture out to catch some local gig action, it was Thursday that made the biggest

**'We all felt like outcasts – that's what brought us all together.' – Gerard Way**

impact on him. Mikey suggested that Gerard meet Geoff Rickly, with a view to him designing some T-shirts for the band. 'I was this hermit artist kid who was Mikey's weird older brother,' recalled Gerard. 'I met Geoff outside of a record store called St. Marks in Kearny, and I remember this really strange-looking kid who looked like he was in Joy Division. He had a black mop; he looked emaciated and pale-as-shit sick. But he was so nice, and we hit it off immediately.'

'Gerard would stay at home,' Rickly told *Kerrang!* 'I got the feeling that he was severely depressed because he would never come out. When I finally met him, we formed a friendship right away. He was a big fan of Thursday and so, in the early days, he did some Thursday T-shirts and things like that.'

'I remember at these parties Gerard coming up to me and being really psyched on Thursday, having seen us and telling some amazing stories about the way it made him feel,' Rickly explained to *Alternative Press* in 2005. 'At the time, I think he was sort of at a low point in his life. He would disappear and not come out for a month and a half.'

Formed in 1997, Thursday had become a feature of the New Jersey scene before signing to Eyeball Records in 1999. Their debut album, *Waiting*, was released that December and established the group's reputation for blending accessible post-hardcore melodies with sensitive lyricism. Thematically, Rickly drew a great deal of inspiration from Joy Division, the legendary post-punk quartet whose lyrics explored a barren landscape of post-industrial alienation and isolation. In addition to Joy Division-influenced song titles such as 'In Transmission', *Waiting* featured a track entitled 'Ian Curtis' – a tribute to the troubled epileptic vocalist who committed suicide in 1980. The song is packed with references to the Manchester group's songs ('24 Hours', 'Atrocity Exhibition', 'Heart And Soul') and climaxes with the line 'Love has torn us apart' – an up-front reference to Joy Division's 1980 single 'Love Will Tear Us Apart'.

THE 21ST CENTURY WILL NOT NOW HAPPEN AS PLANNED

Musically, Thursday's chorus pedal-infused guitar sound was closer to that of the Cure than Joy Division, with Rickly's vulnerable vocals bringing to mind the singing style of Cure frontman Robert Smith. The band's mix of well-chosen influences and new ideas proved a winning formula, particularly with Gerard – who subsequently cited Geoff Rickly as providing him with the inspiration to become a singer. 'Geoff from Thursday inspired me as a person to just get up and do that,' Gerard revealed to the *MetalUnderground* site. 'I've been a fan of music and I've always wanted to be in a band. I just never had the urge to be a frontman until I saw him do it. I was like "You know what? It just seems so incredible and it seems like he's actually making a difference and he was doing something." Right at that moment is when I knew I would do it.'

However, after graduating from the School of Visual Arts in 1999, Gerard began the millennium still harbouring ambitions of breaking into animation or comics. For any newcomer without the right contacts, getting a foot in the door with a major comic book company or animation studio can be a difficult and frustrating process. Unable to make much headway, Gerard withdrew. 'I spent a lot of time holed up in that basment depressed. I found it hard to leave the house. I'd been to art school, got out and realised there were no jobs for me. I went through a lot of negative stuff. I'd sit there beating myself up about not accomplishing anything.'

> 'It's less about the bullies and more about the victory of giving people like us a voice.' – Gerard Way

During this period, Gerard formed a band with his brother called Raygun Jones. Described by Mikey as 'the Smashing Pumpkins meets Weezer', the group was hamstrung by Gerard's increasing tendency to shrink from any kind of social interaction, and quickly disintegrated without performing or recording a proper demo.

Gerard's self-esteem received a welcome boost when he was accepted as an intern at the Cartoon Network. This internship provided Gerard with an environment in which his innate creativity could flourish, and before long he was impressing studio executives with his ideas for new shows. He conceived a series called *The Breakfast Monkey,* which featured a Scandinavian simian superhero who wanted to bring the goodness of breakfast to the world. 'I went from being an intern on a show that was running on Cartoon Network to being someone that was selling a show to them, which bummed a lot of people out because I was the photocopy dude that got a shot,' Gerard recalled. 'But you have to be completely immersed in order for it to be good. You have to live and breathe and shit it, come up with new ideas for shows.'

Assisted by Brooklyn artist Joe Boyle, who handled the inking chores, Gerard progressed his concept to the storyboard stage and the series was optioned by the network. Ultimately, *The Breakfast Monkey* was deemed to be too close to the similarly food-orientated *Aqua Teen Hunger Force*, and the option to produce a series was not picked up. Although this was a disappointment, getting so close to creating his very own animated series at such an early stage proved that Gerard's artistic abilities were more than sufficient to forge a career.

> 'I literally said to myself, "Fuck art. I've gotta get out of the basement. I've gotta see the world. I've gotta make a difference."' – Gerard Way

By 2001, Gerard had produced work for all three of the main comic book publishers, which included 'a bunch of toy designs that I still do for Spider-Man action figures . . . I did a page in DC Comics' *Big Book of the Weird Wild West*, and some *Footsoldiers* work for Image Comics, which was written by my buddy Jim Krueger.' Gerard also began working on a comic book series of his own, *The Amazing Goffo Brothers, Piano Movers Extraordinaire* – a black comedy set in a Kafkaesque metropolis, conceived as a metaphor for his relationship with Mikey. Sadly, *The Amazing Goffo Brothers* remains uncompleted and unpublished, which is a pity as it was in the vein of the more cerebral, progressive comics published by DC's Vertigo imprint. 'I have a wide range of influences with my writing, lyrics and comics,' Gerard told *Comics International* in April 2007. 'Grant Morrison is probably my favourite. That guy has more ideas in his pinkie than most people do in a lifetime, and he doesn't mind tossing them into just one issue.'

Although he found the creative processes of working in comics and animation enjoyable, Gerard quickly became disillusioned with the business aspects of the medium. 'The animation business is even more cutthroat and corrupt than the music industry, I felt like I was throwing my life away.' Gerard reacted to his disenchantment in his usual manner, and spent days on end shut away in his room. 'The positive side was that I ended up with notebooks full of ideas. I even wrote a short story called *I Brought You My Bullets, You Brought Me Your Love*. It was about gangland murders in Chicago. But the point was, I had all these ideas and it meant that I was already shaping an aesthetic for this band – I just didn't have a band yet.'

By the late summer of 2001, Gerard had moved into designing action figures for Marvel. 'That was the last job I had and it was a lot of fun. That was actually probably the best job that I'd ever had. I got to work on a lot of exciting things.' Soon after, Gerard's growing unhappiness with his career path reached critical mass at precisely the moment that – potentially – his biggest break in comics materialised. 'He got the gig from Marvel to do Spider-Man and he bailed on them,' recalled Alex Saavedra. 'Which, to me, was a sign that this kid's really losing his mind – he can't handle it. He gets a gig like that for a company like that, what the hell is he going to do when anything else happens?'

'Basically I wanted to change the direction of my life,' Gerard told the *Chart Attack* website's Pete Richards. 'I wasn't happy with where it was going, I wasn't doing anything important or relevant and I felt kind of useless wasting time in Jersey.'

'So we had an intervention,' explained Saavedra. 'Me, Mikey, Gerard, a couple of our other friends and he started getting better . . . he decided he wanted to start a new band.'

Just as the foundations of a new direction were coalescing in Gerard's mind, the events of 11 September 2001 served to cement his future. 'I was in Hoboken which is right across the Hudson River,' he recalled. 'There was 400 people and me, and I was at the railing. Right in front of us it just went down. It was the biggest fucking neutron bomb of mental anguish you've ever felt. I knew I didn't have anybody in that building, but these were all co-workers and stuff and they were just freaking the fuck out. Crying and screaming and cursing and yelling about the Devil.'

'Something just clicked in my head, and that was when I said, "Fuck art" for the first time,' Gerard told *Rolling Stone*'s Jenny Eliscu. 'I thought, "Art's not doing anything for you. It's just something on a wall, it's completely disposable, and it's not helping anyone." And I was like, "Fuck *Breakfast Monkey*, because all it's gonna do is line somebody else's pockets." I felt like I had given my life to art and that it had betrayed me.' Subsequently, Alex Saavedra testified to the impact 9/11 had on Gerard: 'That really freaked him out – he didn't leave his house for a while.'

> 'I saw Thursday perform at this club for 50 people, and it changed me.' – Gerard Way

'From then on, I was in my parents' basement with a small practice amp and a very old Fender guitar,' explained Gerard in a 2006 *Kerrang!* interview. 'That's when I wrote "Skylines And Turnstiles" and some of the earlier material. I wrote those songs sitting in pyjamas with notebooks all around me. It was me going, "All this stuff has been inside me for years and I want to get it out." I wasn't depressed at that time exactly but I was certainly a hermit.'

The attack on the World Trade Centre had provided Gerard with an impetus to reassess his life. '9/11 made me want to change everything. I took a huge risk with my life after that, because I felt I wasn't helping,' he told *Rock Sound*. 'I went to donate blood, but I got turned away. So I thought, "What can I do? I'm gonna have to find a bunch of dudes that want to speak to people and we're going to do it together."'

> 'We were trying to fulfil some sort of destiny. We felt something calling us. We thought, "Let's start a band."' – Gerard Way

Gerard's resolve to get into music was reinforced when he caught Thursday playing a local show in front of around 50 people. 'He told me one night that Thursday gave him new hope and he was gonna start a band with his little brother,' recalled Geoff Rickly. 'He would sit there and play me songs on one of Alex's guitars that was so hopelessly out of tune and broken with bad strings that I couldn't even tell what he was doing. But I was like, "I love you and your brother, and sure, man; I'll hang out. I'll come to practice."'

The immediate problem facing Gerard in his quest was that neither he, nor Mikey, possessed anything like the technical skills required to perform. His search for 'a bunch of dudes' began with Matt Pelissier, an old friend who had drummed in a number of local bands. 'I ran into Matt at a bar and said, "You know what? I've been writing songs. You're not doing anything, and I'm not doing anything, so let's get together and give it a shot."'

Gerard played Matt a rudimentary version of 'Skylines And Turnstiles' that he had recorded at home. The drummer, also known as 'Otter', was sufficiently impressed with the song to agree to assist Gerard by laying down some drums on a proper demo. Like many aspiring guitarists, Gerard found it difficult to sing and play simultaneously. Opting to concentrate on his natural vocal talents, he decided to recruit a guitarist – the obvious choice being Ray Toro, a mutual friend of both Gerard and Matt – who, like Otter, had previously been a member of Kearny punk outfit the Rodneys. Toro had also worked with the elder Way on a *faux*-country comedy song for *The Breakfast Monkey*. 'That is actually the first collaboration between me and Ray Toro,' confirmed Gerard. 'It predates My Chemical Romance by four months, there's a song called "Cruising For Crazy" that this badly sugar damaged boy who rides a giant goldfish sings – so technically that's the first My Chemical Romance song.'

*The original quintet strike intense poses for one of the band's first publicity shoots.*

Ray's technical prowess was well developed – exactly what Gerard's high enthusiasm/low ability project required. 'Ray was the sort of guy you'd find working in a guitar shop,' observed Geoff Rickly. 'One of those people who'd be a little hard to deal with because he'd be a much better player than anyone else.' Gerard was certainly well aware of Ray's talents. 'He was actually playing drums for a local band at the time. Ray's that kind of guy – he was the best guitar player in Jersey, yet he was playing drums just because he wanted to be playing.'

Keen to involve Toro, Gerard wasted little time in contacting him. 'I talked to him that night and said the same thing I had said to Matt: no strings attached; you don't have to say yes or no. Just come, check it out, and bring your guitar.'

Fortunately, the guitarist was just as impressed with Gerard's rough tape as Matt had been. 'They played me their one song and I was jumping around the attic and head-banging,' Ray told *Blender* in 2005. 'Gerard sounded really sincere about wanting to start something real. That's what made me excited.'

Raymond Manuel Toro-Ortiz was born in Kearny, New Jersey on Friday, 15 July 1977. His childhood had been similar to Gerard and Mikey's in that his parents were loathe to allow him to him play outside, due to the dangers of his immediate neighbourhood. Ray grew up in a small house on the border that straddles the New Jersey towns of Kearny and Harrison, which he shared with his parents and two brothers. 'There was definitely a funny collection of people who would hang around my block,' Ray recounted in an interview with *Alternative Press* journalist Leslie Simon. 'There was this guy named Bertine who was this drug addict, who, every couple of months, would OD outside my house. I would see an ambulance come and take him away.' Indeed, when dead bodies began showing up in nearby West Hudson Park pond, Ray's mother swung into protective mode and insisted he remain indoors.

> 'I'd been feeling lost since I was about 22 because I would always put a lot of pressure on myself, I'd been depressed and the band in many ways was a last ditch effort.' – Gerard Way

Ray's family combine a Puerto Rican and Portuguese heritage, and his father worked in the Post Office shipping department. As a small child he enjoyed playing with his pet dog, but tended to be shy, particularly around new people.

By the time he entered Kearny High School, Ray had inherited a passion for music from his older brother. 'He'd always have a guitar lying around the house and be jamming on it day and night,' Ray told *Epiphone News*' Don Mitchell. 'My mom would get really mad because it would be like two o'clock in the morning and he'd still be playing while we were all trying to sleep. He always had a ton of guitar magazines lying around and books like Pink Floyd and Metallica that had the tabs so I just started picking them up and trying to learn.'

In addition to inspiring him to pick up a guitar, Ray's brother also passed on a palette of influences that would ultimately inform his hard rocking style. 'My brother introduced me to Ozzy's music when I was fourteen, and right away Randy Rhoads became my biggest influence,' Ray recalled in a 2005 interview with *Guitar World*. 'I was inspired by his mix of classical music and metal and started modelling a lot of my playing after his.' As well as tragically deceased guitar hero Rhoads, Ray drew inspiration from the axe heroics of Metallica's Kirk Hammett, Guns N' Roses' Slash and Jimmy Page.

Ray's passion for listening to and playing rock'n'roll quickly became his sole focus. 'I got really obsessed with the guitar,' he explained to *Kerrang!* 'I didn't have much of a social life. I had friends but we wouldn't hang out after school. The only thing that was always there for me was the

> **'I think we were all really in that stage of our lives where we were kind of at that crossroads where you can either go one way or another.' – Ray Toro**

guitar.' In addition to the sort of application that saw him enrol in guitar lessons and a typing course to improve his manual dexterity, it was soon evident he had considerable natural ability as a musician – in direct contrast to his undistinguished performance as a student. 'I was one of the invisible people at school. I didn't excel at anything. I wasn't terrible at anything. After school I would go home alone and sit and play guitar and video games until the next day.'

Unsurprisingly, Ray began hooking up with local bands, the most successful of which were the Rodneys – who formed in 1994 and built a sizeable local following, releasing an album, *Soccertown USA*, in 1997. However, despite this degree of local stardom, on graduating from high school Ray chose film over music and enrolled on an editing course at William Paterson University in Wayne, New Jersey. 'I wanted to be an editor, that was my focus,' he recalled. 'The whole time I was in college learning that, I almost stopped playing in bands. I played drums in a band called Dead Go West for about a year, that was it.'

'Being in a band wasn't really a dream of mine. I always wanted to write music. I enjoy recording more and the process of writing, I never thought that being in a touring band was a possibility,' Ray told *Rock Sound*. 'I enjoyed getting a bunch of scenes and cutting it together so it makes sense. I made one short film about a guy who was obsessed with eating eggs every day. He finally opens up this egg carton and there's one egg left, but he can't crack it open, so he gets driven insane.'

It was Rodneys frontman Shawn Dillon who introduced Ray to Gerard and Mikey during the late 1990s. 'I met Mikey and Gerard a couple of years after I graduated High School,' Ray recalled. 'We were kind of all into the same stuff, like comic books, horror movies and music . . . It was a very quick friendship with everybody.'

Initially, Ray was closer to Mikey than his less sociable older brother. 'Gerard was like this introverted artist that never really left the house,' recalled the guitarist on the *Life On The Murder Scene* DVD. 'Over the years of me knowing him, I rarely saw him . . . I really didn't see him maybe except for in his house and later at the practice studio.'

After agreeing to hook up with Gerard and Matt, Ray settled into the practice sessions and quickly realised the trio shared an almost instinctive creative chemistry. 'After a while it became obvious that there was an energy we all felt when we were playing together and that's how we started,' he observed.

> **'We always had a vision, but we weren't sure if it would translate or just come off as pretentious.' – Mikey Way**

At this stage, the band was without either a name or a bassist. The solution to both deficiencies arrived in the form of Mikey. Gerard, Ray and Matt had recorded a demo in Matt's attic. 'It was a wooden, run-down piece of crap,' the drummer explained in an interview for *Alternative Press*. 'I had a really cheap sixteen-track board, and we had a bunch of crappy mics. I basically had the drums and guitars playing upstairs and ran mics down the stairs and had Gerard sing in the bathroom.'

The tape included a new version of 'Skylines And Turnstiles' as well as basic renditions of 'Cubicles' and 'Our Lady Of Sorrows' – which at that stage was called 'Bring More Knives'. 'You could hear that it was something really new, and it was kind of a weird idea, but for some reason, as poorly as it was coming together, it really worked,' enthused Gerard. 'And a lot of people loved the demo.'

Chief among the new band's admirers was Mikey, who – egged on by Alex Saavedra – dropped out of college in order to learn bass guitar and join his brother in the group. 'It's funny, because before Mikey was in My Chem, I was gonna play bass,' recalled Saavedra. 'But I already had another band that I was really stoked on.'

In late 2001, Mikey's only previous musical experience was an unsuccessful audition to join Eyeball combo Pencey Prep. 'Mikey already knew how to play guitar a little bit – he wasn't very good at all, so he didn't know how to play bass either,' explained Saavedra. 'At first, it was just everybody teaching him how to play bass, teaching him how to tune it – which is hilarious to think about 'cos Mikey just really didn't know how to play it. But it's

Gerard's brother and one of our best friends, so we knew that he needed to be involved.'

Despite his lack of technical knowledge, Mikey's enthusiasm became an important ingredient in the band's early development. 'Mikey is the eternal kid brother of the band. He has a lot of heart and is just a bit shy and awkward. We're very protective of him.' To support himself, the novice bassist had taken a job stacking shelves at a local branch of Barnes and Noble. 'One dark and stormy night, someone left a stack of Irvine Welsh novels on the ground. The words "Chemical Romance" caught my eye,' Mikey told the *Teenspot* website.

Adding the prefix 'My' to give the name 'a personal touch', Mikey had hit upon the perfect name for his new band. 'The name "My Chemical Romance" originated from the author Irvine Welsh's novel *Three Tales of Chemical Romance*,' he explained. 'All of Irving Welsh's novels have also been classified as "Chemical Romances" as they involved young people whom are strung out on drugs with some sort of romantic element to it. This isn't to say that the band condones drug use, as we are all clean and sober.'

'We really just wanted a name that wouldn't sound like any other,' recalled Gerard. 'There are a lot of trends in names right now. We tried to stay away from that. We went through five or six different names, a couple of them are actually band names now with different bands.'

With the name universally accepted, the band now had an identity to go along with a full compliment of singers and players. In addition to this, the feelings of rejection and isolation that Gerard, Mikey and Ray had experienced as adolescents served to give the group a purpose. 'We were the lowest of the low,' insisted Gerard. 'We came from a crappy area, and though there are lots of nice apartments in New Jersey, that wasn't us. This is for every moment we were ever picked on at school. It feels like our destiny, as individuals and together as a band. It wasn't a bitter revenge, just something we always focussed on. It was like there was an invisible enemy we wanted revenge against.'

'We were originally united as a group because we ourselves were obvious outsiders,' Gerard told *Metal Hammer* in 2006. 'We were pretty much invisible and insignificant. When nobody pays any attention to you, you realise how mortal you are. That's why teenagers that are troubled or are seen as outcasts are drawn to death. You have a lot of time to examine that subject when you're all alone.'

Now all My Chemical Romance had to do was get up on stage and find their public.

# Chapter 3

# THE BROTHERHOOD OF DADA

**'There is something so honest about youth and I think that a band that is honest and sincere connects with that.'**
**– Gerard Way**

Barely a month after forming, Gerard, Mikey, Ray and Matt nervously made their way onto a cramped, makeshift stage at the VFW hall in Ewing, New Jersey. Headliners that night were Pencey Prep, already veterans of the local basement gig circuit, whose debut album, *Heartbreak In Stereo*, was set for an imminent release on Eyeball. In keeping with the inclusive nature of the scene, Pencey Prep offered their novice openers plenty of support, advice and encouragement. Prep bassist John 'Hambone' McGuire gave My Chem a morale-boosting talk as they took Dutch courage before squeezing onto the venue's modest stage. One huge, collective intake of breath later, the band launched into 'Skylines And Turnstiles'.

As audiences go, a gathering of less than 50 barely qualifies as a 'crowd'. However, in the tight confines of a hall more used to hosting the cathartic confessions of recovering alcoholics than the latest thing in rock'n'roll, the neophyte quartet could be forgiven for imagining they were playing to an army of rabid fans as those gathered exploded into a kinetic mass of flailing arms and arching spines. 'The room just blew up,' Gerard told *Kerrang!* in 2006. 'It was the best first gig we could possibly have had. We played the rest of the set on this wave; we felt totally on fire.'

*Gerard Way – bulletproof punk.*

The unexpected fervour from those fortunate enough to witness My Chemical Romance's live debut burned off the quartet's pre-show nerves, in a searing jet-stream of spontaneous approval. The compressed energy bounced back and forth between band and audience, generating a compression chamber of supercharged excitement. 'It felt so good,' enthused Mikey. 'It was like we were part of something. I was thinking, "Something's going to happen here, I can feel it." It felt like a spark on a pile of woodchips.'

> 'I knew Gerard as the comic-book artist, as Mikey's creepy older brother.' – Frank Iero

Encouraged beyond their wildest imaginings, the quartet began the arduous task of establishing an identity and a fanbase among the Jersey scene. 'The first places we played were VFW halls,' recalled Ray. 'In Jersey, bands put on shows in VFW halls and they'll charge maybe $5 or $6 for a show that has five or six local bands on the bill. They were usually really small shows where like ten to fifteen kids would show up or maybe 40 if you were lucky. It was really fun though.'

Regardless of the size of the audience, early MCR shows were characterised by the passion with which the group attacked their short sets. 'I had never moved around onstage when I had played in bands before – I had always just stood there,' explained Ray. 'This time, the music made me headbang and thrash around. I was wild onstage and I had never experienced that before.'

'We just went out there and tried to destroy things,' Gerard recalled in a 2005 interview with *Rolling Stone*. 'I didn't want people to stand there and look at it like it was art. We wanted it to be explosive and cathartic.'

Despite these early successes on their home turf, one of My Chemical Romance's first shows away from New Jersey saw them billed as 'the Chemical Brothers' by a befuddled Philadelphia promoter. 'We didn't even draw as the Chemical Brothers,' laughed Mikey. 'It was one of our first shows, and I'm sure people knew that the Chemical Brothers weren't playing the Fire.'

Even before My Chem's gigography had reached double figures, it was apparent that they were not a run-of-the-mill basement band. Their local crowds responded to them in an immediate and partisan manner – it was as if the band had stepped from the mosh pit onto the stage and delivered a set that encapsulated the Jersey scene and the kids that made it happen. Without contrivance or artifice, this band *were* the kids. There was no arrogance, hubris or hierarchy surrounding MCR – just powerful, catchy songs that reflected the lives of both the group and those they were playing to.

Pencey Prep guitarist Frank Iero was among the first to realise that something big was brewing in the Garden State. 'Me and my band were like, "Wow, this band's going to do something,"' he told *Metal Edge* magazine. 'We didn't know what it was, and we didn't know if they were going to be, like, the biggest band in the world, or if they were just going to make one record and flop, but change the way a lot of kids think. Either way, they were going to do *something* big.'

The guitarist had also heard MCR's demo tape. 'Oh man, that thing was so shitty, but there was something about it and nobody knew what it was,' he recalled in a 2005 *Revolver* interview. 'It's not together, nothing is in tune, but you could always imagine what it would sound like put together properly. My band at the time would listen to the demo on the way to and from our shows, and it would get us psyched up. I became a huge fan and good friends with the guys.'

> '**I wasn't popular at school. Thank God I didn't have a girlfriend or I would suck at guitar now.' – Ray Toro**

Iero's friendship with My Chem soon developed into something far more significant and enduring, when the band decided their sound could do with fattening up by adding a second guitarist; with Pencey Prep beginning to unravel, Frank became the obvious candidate. He was asked to join and accepted without hesitation. 'I knew this is it; this is what I need to do,' he told *Detroit Free Press* journalist Brian McCollum. 'I dropped everything, got in a van and never looked back. I got crying phone calls from my parents – "You need to go back to school!" I said, "You don't understand. This is something I need. I need to be here." That's the way I've felt about this band since day one.'

'It was fucking awesome,' Frank enthused in *Kerrang!* 'I felt like the kid in the crowd who had been pulled up to play a song. I just *loved* the band.'

Born on Saturday, 31 October 1981, Frank was My Chemical Romance's junior member. Of all those in the band, Frank's musical background was the most clearly delineated – his father was an accomplished drummer who also taught at local schools and clinics, and his grandfather had played in Dixieland jazz ensembles for many years. 'I just remember growing up, listening to them talk about gigs that they had played or people that they played with or where they're playing next,' Frank recalled in an interview with Mike Pasaretti of *Punkbands.com*. 'It was amazing. It was the main thing at the dinner table and at holidays. I just knew early on that that was what I needed to do; it was part of my family, it was in my blood. Growing up, my father would get me interested in his music – blues, old rock, and stuff like that.'

Like Gerard and Mikey, Frank grew up in Belleville, where his opportunities to go out and mix with other kids were even more limited than his future bandmates on account of his poor health. A slight child, Frank suffered from constant bronchitis and was prone to ear infections that necessitated regular hospital visits.

The flames of what would grow into a burning passion for music were nurtured in Frank by his father, who, in addition to teaching and playing in several local ensembles, had racked up session time with John Lennon, Iggy Pop and Kiss. 'My dad would ask me how school was, but mostly it was, "When are you going to start playing?"'

> 'So many people treat you like you're a kid so you might as well act like one and throw your television out of the hotel window.' – Gerard Way

'My father would sneak me into clubs so I could watch him,' Frank told *Rock Sound*. 'I was always doing something – loading gear or whatever. I'd see my dad up there and I was like, "I have to do it." My family would be talking over dinner and he'd say, "I may not be able to see you next week because I'm playing."'

Inspired by this early exposure to the rock'n'roll lifestyle, Frank quickly became determined to extend the Iero family's musical lineage. His ambitions began to solidify when his father took him to see folk guitarist Richie Havens play an intimate show. 'I've never seen anyone play guitar like that – the passion he had behind it and the way he was strumming, he had an incredible rhythmic sense and told these stories of things he'd seen and stories behind the songs he was writing, and how he had met Bob Dylan and things like that. Listening to him speak, and how he felt about his music and how he felt about the songs, it inspired me. That's how I knew I wanted to play guitar.'

Although having a musician for a father was a definite advantage so far as Frank's aspirations were concerned, the demands of life on the road ensured there were periods when Linda, Frank's mother, was left alone to bring up her young son. This situation was exacerbated when the couple decided to separate. 'My parents split up when I was pretty young,' Frank explained. 'My mom was kind of left to take care of everything.

There were times when we really couldn't even afford milk.'

'My mom went without to provide for me when I was little, and I still, to this day, don't know how she did it,' Frank told *Metal Edge* in 2005. 'Even when I didn't believe anything was going to happen with what I was doing, she did. She was definitely my rock.' However, despite the separation, Frank's father contributed to his upbringing and continued to provide his son with musical guidance. 'We weren't rich,' he explained to *Kerrang!* 'But my mom tried really hard to make sure I had everything I needed, while my dad worked three jobs to support us.'

By the time he was ten years old, Frank had developed into a clever, if rebellious kid. 'I was such an asshole,' he declared in an interview for the *Trouble Bunch Music* site. 'I was told I was too intelligent for my own good but I don't know about that. I didn't like authority.'

Frank's anti-authoritarianism seeped into his selected listening. He began veering away from the classic blues that his father had introduced him to, toward such rebellious bands as Sonic Youth, Black Flag and Nirvana, whose third and final studio album, *In Utero*, made a huge impression on the aspiring guitarist. 'It was so eye opening,' Frank recounted. 'Through it I found out about bands like Big Black and other guitar players like Greg Ginn and Thurston Moore. Basically, it helped me discover the underground hardcore and punk scenes . . . *In Utero* changed the way I thought about playing guitar. It made me realise that you don't have to play like Van Halen; you just have to play from the heart and put your personality and emotion into it.'

The all-pervading early 1990s influence of Nirvana was much in evidence when Frank made his performing debut, with a set that included the Seattle trio's 1991 b-side 'Aneurysm'. 'I played this song the first time I ever played in a band in front of people,' he recalled. 'I was about twelve and we didn't have enough songs of our own, so we had to cover this.'

'I was never much for cock rock virtuoso guitar players,' Frank explained to Darin Longman of the *Iowa State Daily*. 'I like metal but it wasn't something that I was inspired to play. I wanted to be Thurston Moore. I wanted to be a normal guy who put his emotions through a guitar. If you study hard enough, you can play scales at light speed, but nobody can ever mimic what Thurston Moore does. Those bands were the ones that made me want to play.'

Throughout middle school, Frank devoted the bulk of his free time to honing his skills and soon began hooking up with groups of pals to form bedroom bands. 'I've been in bands since I was eleven years old and my parents have always been supportive,' he recalled. 'They always let me practice in the basement with my band and as long as I was doing well in school I could play as many shows as I wanted.' Like his future bandmates, Frank found that his lack of enthusiasm for mainstream pursuits led to him being marginalised at high school. Like Gerard, Mikey and Ray, Frank was a tabloid textbook outsider, into rock, metal and horror movies. 'I grew up on candy corn, pumpkins, and horror movies like *The Texas Chainsaw Massacre* and *Dawn of the Dead*,' Frank explained. 'I wanted to do special effects for movies.'

Frank attended the Catholic Queen of Peace High School in Arlington, which was a five-minute bus ride from his home. 'I had about three friends,' he remembered. 'I didn't do much, I'd get really high and that was about it. I didn't really want to be in school. I wanted to play music but I was always told that wouldn't work. I got bullied a lot too.'

At 5'4", Frank would be the shortest member of MCR, and his diminutive stature made him an easy target for bullies. 'We didn't really fit in among the cool kids at school,' he told the University of Southern California's student paper, the *Daily Trojan*. 'We were constantly searching for acceptance. I definitely found that in being in a band. It just felt like that's where my place was in this world.

## 'I wouldn't change my upbringing for the world.' – Frank Iero

'I would go see local shows all the time because I felt that it was my music,' explained Frank. '[It was] made by kids like me, the shows were put on by kids and there were kids attending the shows. I felt like I could do that.'

Despite his focus on music, Frank's natural intellect ensured he graduated from high school with sufficient grades to secure a place at Rutgers University. However, as his success in local bands began to snowball, his studies quickly took a very withdrawn back seat. Towards the end of his time in high school, Frank had formed Sector 12, who gigged regularly and built up a small local following. Once he was at university he teamed up with John 'Hambone' McGuire, a bassist friend who had supplied Frank with a steady stream of punk compilation tapes, to form Pencey Prep. The name of the band was derived from the school that Holden Caulfield attended in J. D. Salinger's 1951 novel, *The Catcher in the Rye*. During 1999, the band set about honing their mix of punk and alt-rock with nightly practice sessions in Frank's basement, and made their live debut in 2000, supporting New York indie trio Nada Surf at the Loop Lounge in Passaic Park, New Jersey.

Pencey Prep began gigging extensively on the New Jersey basement club circuit, where their performances were notable for Frank's whole-hearted approach to performing. 'He gave it everything, he was a fantastic front man,' recalled McGuire. 'Our whole band was insepa-

*Out in the cold – the misfits who rocked the world.*

rable. We'd rehearse for nine hours a day, go to a show, then go back and rehearse some more.'

The band's exciting live shows ensured they soon fell under the gaze of Eyeball Records, who released a debut single, 'Yesterday'/'Lloyd Dobbler', in early 2001, and the band's only album, *Heartbreak In Stereo,* in November of the same year. Sadly, the group split just as the album was released, and Frank capped an eventful month by joining My Chemical Romance, with whom they had shared a rehearsal space. 'When that band broke up our first instinct was to get him,' observed Ray. 'He was already a fan of our band and a great guitar player.'

Gerard was equally delighted to have the guitarist in the band. 'Frank is an extremely passionate, headstrong, kind of rebellious individual but extremely loyal and honest, the kind of guy that would do anything for his friends.' He told *Zero* magazine. 'He's the guy that would help you bury the body.'

The addition of Frank to the roster bolstered My Chem's technical expertise and concert experience quotients considerably, and the group wasted little time in solidifying their sound through constant rehearsal and a steady stream of live shows. 'We played basements, legion halls, anywhere, as often as we could,' recalled Frank. 'I even played a hot-dog stand once. We'd play anywhere, 'cos it's all we had.'

MCR's fusion of influences served to position the band in a unique niche, not conforming to the prevalent emo or hardcore templates, but with a sound that referenced elements of both sub-genres. The absence of an obvious stylistic pigeonhole had a polarising effect on the band's early audiences; whereas there was often a small knot of people singing along with the set, there was also a sizeable proportion of the crowd who would opt to stand back, snipe, heckle and jeer. Such negative reactions go with the support band's territory – however, on many occasions the small but enthusiastic My Chem following found themselves set upon by fans of other acts. 'That would happen every night,' Frank explained to *Metal Hammer*. 'It was quite a disheartening time.'

'People at the very beginning would call us faggots and stuff like that,' Gerard told *Big Cheese*. 'We were being discriminated against from very early on. The minute you open your mouth to stand up for yourself or to say something different from what everyone else is saying people will start hating you. You pose a threat to them. People don't like it and this band is a very threatening thing to a lot of people and that's the beauty of it.'

## 'I think that the music we create together is one of a kind.' – Ray Toro

My Chem's belief in their creative direction enabled them to overcome abuse from audiences who hadn't come along specifically to see them and drew the quintet into a tightly knit gang. 'You start to realise that the people that are with you are your best friends,' observed Frank. 'We've always felt like it was us versus the world. Especially early on, when we were on the bad tours and going to these shows where no one gave a shit about us. You go into this show and people want to hate you. We would go in there and we knew it was us versus everyone in that room; that was just the mentality that we had going into it.'

The siege mentality adopted by My Chem in the face of gales of belligerent scorn from those Gerard identified as 'suburban quarterback punk rock kids' spread to the band's increasingly partisan local fanbase, who began to demonstrate a near evangelical zeal. 'Those kids would photocopy flyers for our local shows and go to other Jersey shows and put them on cars, guerrilla style,' declared Mikey. 'It all began with those kids.'

The unique nature of the New Jersey scene combined with My Chemical Romance's unshakable belief, and the unwavering support of their followers, to allow the band to operate outside of the traditional industry processes. 'We didn't use any "music business" advice at all,' Gerard told *Grind* magazine. 'We created what we wanted. We made something that we felt didn't exist. We made our own world, we live in a bubble and it's ours 'cos we built it and we were able to make the music we felt was missing, that we really wanted to hear.'

My Chem also embraced the potential of online technology as a means of spreading the word, setting up a website and MySpace page to showcase their songs and promote gigs. 'We kind of anti-promoted,' Gerard recalled in a 2005 interview with the *Pollstar* website's Tina Amendola. 'We would play shows and not say our name. We didn't make stickers, we didn't have merch. The first thing we had was a web site. I just felt like we were doing this for a reason.'

The band's 'net presence proved to be an ideal marketing medium, allowing A&R people to check the group out without having to get down and dirty at a live show. 'When we put our first song up on the internet, within weeks we had record company A&R men knocking on our door and wanting us to sign record contracts and reign us in for life,' Mikey revealed in an interview for Australian website *Fasterlouder.com*. 'We said "no" because we just wanted to let the band be a band and see how we could evolve without other people telling us what to do.'

Rather than submit to the marketing whims of a major label intent on packaging the band as a replication of the latest big thing, My Chem reciprocated the interest of Eyeball Records, who had already established their credibility through Frank's experiences of the label with Pencey Prep and Mikey's internship. 'We had recorded a demo with my computer that was just kind of slapped together in a day or two,' explained Ray. 'It sounded really crappy but Alex liked the songs and wanted to help us out so he put us in a small studio in New York. We recorded one track and at that time we had never recorded with even half-way decent equipment so when we finished that track we were totally stoked.'

On the strength of that session and their incendiary local shows, Alex Saavadra offered to fund the recording of an album to be released on Eyeball. Within three months of playing their first show, My Chemical Romance had landed a record deal. It was a huge opportunity for the rookie quintet, but also brought considerable pressure for them to fulfil the expectations of their already committed followers.

# Chapter 4

# LIKE GHOSTS IN THE SNOW

## 'I didn't feel like I had any control over my life and this gave me control back.'
## – Gerard Way

The wet, windswept start to 2002 saw My Chemical Romance begin their career as recording artists. The band checked into the Nada Recording Studio in upstate New York, just over an hour's drive north from Belleville. Owned by producer/engineer John Naclerio, the small, well-equipped facility had played host to a steady stream of bands from New York and New Jersey since its opening in 1995. Accompanying the group was Geoff Rickly, who had offered to produce the album, with some assistance from Eyeball mainman Alex Saavedra.

The rapidity with which My Chem landed an album deal represented a double-edged sword: on one hand, it was an unmissable opportunity to establish their creative credentials and expand their audience – alternatively, the band's collective lack of experience meant they'd not yet built up a huge set list from which to cherry-pick road-tested songs for their debut. 'We knew what we had was very kind of new, and very exciting and very inventive. It still needed to be banged into shape, we thought,' explained Gerard in an interview with *Cincinnati City Beat*'s Alan Sculley. 'We were only three months in, so we were still trying to figure out who we were.'

Having hooked up with his new bandmates less than a month earlier, Frank was

*Guitarist Ray Toro takes centre stage for a November 2005 publicity shoot.*

keenly aware that he was being thrown in at the deep end. 'I was probably only in the band actually three weeks before working on that record. And I remember sitting in a van outside with no heat trying to write parts to songs that we were about to record because I hadn't been in the band long enough to actually write things for it.'

Additionally, the newly teamed twin-guitar pairing of Frank and Ray had to work out how to accommodate each other's playing during the recording sessions. 'I wished we had had more time,' lamented Ray. 'I had never played with another guitarist before and he brought a very different style and way of thinking to the band.'

> 'Lots of people inspired me, and I put them all into a stew and distilled it.' – Gerard Way

In normal circumstances, any rookie band's first experience in a studio provides a steep learning curve; for MCR this curve edged rapidly towards the vertical, as they struggled to get to grips with their newly expanded line-up and expand their corpus of recordable material. The experience that Saavedra and Rickly brought to the situation quickly proved invaluable, as their encouragement and expertise helped temper the fraught early sessions. 'I remember one time in the studio, saying to Gerard, "Dude, seriously, you know how much bigger you're going to be than Thursday?" and he started blushing and being like, "Stop it, dude, I have confidence. You don't need to tell me ridiculous stuff like that,"' recalled Rickly. 'Now, I call him, and I'm like, "Remember when I told you that?" I just had no idea it was going to be *this* big.'

Reflecting on Rickly's reason for offering to produce the album, Gerard observed, 'I think he wanted to be involved because it didn't sound like them. The cool thing about Eyeball is they don't sign bands that sound like Thursday. We work pretty close at their office, we'll do our mail order sometimes, and we just try to help them. There are only two guys, Marc and Alex, who run it. They do a ton of fucking work. They get a ton of demos all the time. Everyone of them sounds exactly like Thursday. And they sign none of them.'

Unsurprisingly, given the obstacles set before them, the early days at Nada Studio went fairly poorly, with Gerard becoming increasingly uncomfortable, depressed, and immobilised by a series of severe headaches. 'I had all these thoughts of ending my life, but they were just thoughts,' he revealed to *Revolver* magazine. 'For a while, I was on Wellbutrin for depression, and you can't drink or you get an aneurysm. But I didn't listen at first, and I had some serious migraines. I thought my head was going to explode.'

Crisis point arrived early – during the recording of hit song 'Vampires Will Never

Hurt You', which was the first track to be committed to tape. 'Gerard was getting very frustrated because it was his first time recording, decently, in an actual studio. He was overwhelmed and he was over-thinking it,' Saavedra told *Alternative Press.* 'So I punched him in the face! The blow loosened Gerard's jaw and somehow gave him the motivation to take to the mic and rip a bite out of the track.'

'I remember it hurting a lot, and going, "All right, I hope I can do this,"' recalled Gerard. 'I remember singing, and something clicked. I remember Alex's face was just amazed that the song was finally coming together. I think it was the second take that we ended up using.'

Saavedra's well-aimed punch broke the tense inertia that had plagued MCR, and the remaining ten tracks that would make up the album were laid down in an impressively rapid nine days. 'I think the experience itself in making the record and getting to hang out with Geoff and Alex and John . . . it was just a great experience for us all and we're always going to look at that record as being special,' beamed a delighted Gerard. 'We only did it in like nine days or ten days, something like that. But it was such a great experience and we love everything about the record.'

**'We basically have four punk rock dudes, backed up by a really great guitarist, and it sounds really technical.' – Gerard Way**

During May, John Naclerio mixed the album at Nada, with the final results surpassing the expectations of all involved. 'Geoff told me the first time that he had heard it, he was fucking terrified of what we were capable of,' Gerard enthused. 'It was definitely an incredible experience,' observed Ray. 'It was the first time I think any of us had gone in to record fucking for real, and it sounded so fucking good. We were blown away. We were like whoa, that's us. It was awesome.'

'I told them after their first record that they were gonna be much bigger than Thursday,' Rickly explained to *Spin.* 'We're flip sides of a coin. He [Gerard] deals in the surreal and make-believe and is able to project a confidence that I can't. He has this other place where he can hide and control things. Gerard's always telling me that he's my villain. But I think he's an antihero.'

Described by *Metal Hammer* as 'A hard-hitting punk rock explosion', *I Brought You My Bullets, You Brought Me Your Love* begins unexpectedly, with a spot of classical Spanish guitar. Demonstrating the type of unconventional theatricality that the group would later

I Brought You My Bullets, You Brought Me Your Love –
*My Chem's genre-defying debut.*

establish as part of their style, the brief instrumental 'Romance' grabbed the listener's attention by derailing preconceptions about the content of the disc. Also known as 'Spanish Romance', the piece is based upon a traditional Spanish melody and has long been a staple of classical guitar lessons. The song came to widespread popular attention in 1952 when it was arranged by renowned Murcian guitarist Narciso Yepes, for his soundtrack to René Clément's Oscar–nominated film *Jeux Inderdits* (Forbidden Games). My Chem would subsequently perform the song live, with Gerard improvising lyrics.

The album's sedate opening is immediately juxtaposed by the coruscating twin-guitar assault of 'Honey, This Mirror Isn't Big Enough For The Two Of Us', a churning slice of pop/punk embellished by smart time changes. The song was selected to be the band's debut single and released in tandem with the LP. Only limited numbers of the original Eyeball single were pressed, and the disc now changes hands on internet auction sites and at collectors' fairs for hundreds of dollars. Gerard's vocal delivery is a bilious indictment of his lyrical target – a manipulative, cocaine-addicted former lover, loosely based on an ex-girlfriend of Mikey's.

Directed by Eyeball Records general manager Marc Debiak, the video to 'Honey, This Mirror Isn't Big Enough For The Two Of Us' was a homage to controversial Japanese film maker Takeshi Miike's visceral 1999 revenge thriller, *Audition*. Like the movie, Debiak's excellent video depicts an oriental female torturing her paralysed male victim, deftly intercut with an energetic performance of the song. Not widely seen until 2005, the promo was an imaginatively cinematic screen debut for both director and band.

Debiak also directed a video for 'Vampires Will Never Hurt You'; this time, the smart-suited quintet emerge white-faced from the gloom of a claustrophobic, darkened room to gear-change rapidly through progressively intense states of mania. The small set had been painted black by Gerard and Frank, who got high on, and then became sick from the fumes. Although the song was subsequently described by the *Guardian*'s Caroline Sullivan as 'the juiciest tune the Ramones never wrote', 'Vampires' is far more complex than 'Da Brudders' minimalist punk, with Gerard's frenzied vocal delivery unintentionally evoking Killing Joke's frontman, Jaz Coleman.

Despite his love of the horror genre, Gerard's lyrical use of 'Vampires' was not literal: 'We use vampires as a metaphor for something else, something deeper than just the supernatural,' he explained. 'There are really so many people trying to get control over you on a daily basis and steal your soul in some way, take a part of you.'

A soaring exploration of doomed lovers locked together in an unbreakable circle of desire and death, 'Drowning Lessons' (which had previously been known as 'Wish You Away') showcases the top end of Gerard's vocal range. His lyrics mention 'A thousand bodies piled up' – foreshadowing the vocalist's 'thousand evil men' who would be a key thematic element of the more conceptual second album, *Three Cheers For Sweet Revenge.*

Originally included on the band's first demo as 'Bring More Knives', 'Our Lady Of Sorrows' is a searing slice of punk, in the vein of such early eighties hardcore groups such as the Descendents, Minor Threat and the Adolescents. Lyrically, the track comprises several elements

> **'Everybody wanted to hate us. But we always had in our mind that we wanted to transcend this. We wanted to change the world.' – Mikey Way**

that would soon become established as the core of MCR's ethos: the unity of friendship; the importance of standing up for oneself and one's beliefs; the theme of revenge is introduced into the band's canon for the first time. 'I've been obsessed with revenge ever since I heard the Black Flag song "Revenge",' Gerard told *Kerrang!* 'We thought we could get even for all the shit that's happened to us in our lives, for being raised by good parents in a really bad area. Revenge that meant we could break out. Most of all revenge on all the people who never believed in us.'

Bursting out with a solo plucked straight from the Brian May guitar handbook, 'Headfirst For Halos' switches pace and settles into the kind of shambolic hook that the

Libertines built an enduring cult upon. The pharmaceutical emphasis of Gerard's lyrics is equally reminiscent of Pete Doherty and Carl Bârat's writing. 'I think that what's romantic about us and the Libertines is we're completely exposed, there's no pretence, nothing phoney about it and for better or worse, it is what it is,' Gerard told *New Musical Express* in 2005. 'Obviously we're different – we were able to overcome some chemical addictions and unfortunately for Pete, it doesn't look like he was.' The track is a kind of 'White Rabbit' for the prescription kids of the ADHD generation, with the line, 'Now the red ones make me fly, and the blue ones help me fall' reminiscent of song-writer-vocalist Grace Slick's 'One pill makes you larger/And one pill makes you small,' from Jefferson Airplane's 1967 psychedelic reworking of the *Alice in Wonderland* mythos.

> **'I would get wasted for a show, then need to shut my brain off at night – because my brain is always moving at a million miles a minute.' – Gerard Way**

'That song wrote itself,' declared Gerard. 'In like ten minutes, lyrics, everything. We were just joking around and I was like, this is the catchiest, poppiest, stupidest shit I have ever heard, and I was like, how can I make lyrics make it not? And then I figured a way to do that. At first we were like no, this is not a My Chemical Romance song, but we just kept fighting it until it was.'

The oldest song in My Chem's repertoire, 'Skylines And Turnstiles' is Gerard's lyrical response to witnessing the destruction of the World Trade Centre. It is a raw reaction, filled with jagged time-signature changes and anguished lyrics, delivered with breathless urgency. Although the ambitious arrangement is slightly awkward in parts, and some of the lyrics don't quite scan, the strength of emotion evident in lines such as, 'This broken city sky like butane on my skin and stolen from my eyes' carries the song home.

'Early Sunsets Over Monroeville' sees Gerard digging back into his deep mine of cinematic influences, to unearth a set of lyrics based on George A. Romero's apocalyptic 1978 zombie classic *Dawn of the Dead* – much of which was filmed at the Monroeville Mall in Pennsylvania. Musically, the track is an impressive exercise in restrained energy, with Ray and Frank's subtle guitar interplay suggesting a pastoral ballad as opposed to a

*Less than a month after joining the band, guitarist Frank Iero was thrown in at the deep end as the band recorded their debut album.*

dark exploration of the living dead. Rather than explode into thrashing punk/metal axe mayhem, the six-string duo maintain the melody for the entire song, allowing Gerard to provide the punk dynamics by means of his progressively demonstrative vocal delivery. By the time the number reaches its final verse, you can almost hear his larynx shredding.

Live favourite 'This Is The Best Day Ever' increases the pace towards escape velocity, as the group bounce between no-nonsense thrash and poppier segments. Again, the track features some tricky time changes, and at certain points Matt's drumming accelerates unilaterally. When asked about Matt's drumming for Chrome Dreams' unauthorised DVD documentary, *Things That Make You Go Mmmm*, John Naclerio observed, 'He was the weakest link in the band – he couldn't keep the tempo going.' Lyrically, Gerard explores doomed love set before a backdrop of hospitals and urban decay. The medical motif soon became a regular feature of the frontman's writing. 'With me personally I am in and out of freakin' hospitals constantly and emergency rooms especially, for God knows what,' Gerard told the *Punknews* site. 'So many different things, and all of us are in the hospital or sick, or so many things, and the hospital is just a good metaphor for a lot of stuff. It's kinda a safe place but yet a scary place so I kinda put it in the songs as a metaphor.'

> 'You either get this band or you don't.' – Gerard Way

Another of the band's early songs, 'Cubicles', makes an appearance as the album's penultimate track. An exploration of the empty misery of being stuck in a tedious office environment, surrounded by demoralised co-workers, as real life passes by outside, the track is a fuzz-infused dissection of the human cost of corporate capitalism.

'Demolition Lovers' closes the album. Ambitious and grandiose, the song slowly climbs through successive layers of intensity before hitting a dramatic false climax. The extended coda begins subtly, in the style of 'Early Sunsets Over Monroeville'. However, this time around Ray lets rip with an extended solo that ushers in Gerard's final, fraught visualisation of an ill-starred *Bonnie and Clyde/Natural Born Killers*-style romance.

Unlike MCR's subsequent albums, the songs on *I Brought You My Bullets, You Brought Me Your Love* are unified by Gerard's lyrics and vocals rather than any integrated concept or resolute adherence to a certain sound. 'The first record is a band discovering who it is,' Gerard observed.

Although their debut drew inevitable comparisons with Thursday on account of the involvement of Geoff Rickly and the two groups' origins amid the Jersey basement scene, *I Brought You My Bullets . . .* is an essentially accessible album, in which My Chem's broad palate of influences are fully explored. Subsequent reviewers noted that elements of such diverse acts as Morrissey, Iron Maiden and the Misfits were in evidence, as the quintet crammed a huge variety of music styles onto the disc while managing to maintain overall cohesion. 'Each song is a story unto itself,' Gerard explained in an interview with *Suicide Girls*' Daniel Robert Epestein. 'I'm a big fan of guys like Tom Waits and Nick Cave who are both storytellers. At the time when we put out that record I had a sense that there was a lack of story in lyrics, at least in modern punk, it was mainly stuff about heartbreak. The first album was more autobiographical with me trying to get a lot of crap out of me.'

> **'I think we're a pretty sexy band.' – Frank Iero**

Much of Gerard's lyricism was an exercise in catharsis that enabled him to deal with what he identified as, 'the post-traumatic stress disorder of 9/11, my own shortcomings, being depressed and being suicidal.' To this end, he had developed a straightforward, organic method of composition. 'What I usually do is write paragraphs of free style, just really descriptive phrases and I'll draw upon those phrases later,' he explained to *concertlivewire.com*'s Phil Bonyata and Karen Bondowski. 'Just simple descriptives and adjectives and things like that. Things that sound good together, that look good together, sound and make the picture look good. But I mainly just free style. I try to get the sound before I get the lyrics 'cause even though lyrics are the important thing, the most important thing is the sound that you are communicating.'

The 23 July 2002 release of *I Brought You My Bullets* . . . was marked by a record release party at Maxwell's in Hoboken, New Jersey. The packed show gave My Chemical Romance the sort of reception usually afforded conquering heroes, and kicked off a marathon bout of touring in support of the album. 'As soon as we finished the first record, like a month or two after that we started touring and we really haven't stopped,' recalled Ray in 2004. As Alex Saavedra observed: 'Their lifestyle changed as soon as that record dropped – they were gone.'

# Chapter 5

# THE BAND THAT ATE EMO

**'At one point we sought to destroy emo.
I think we've done a pretty good job of that.'
– Gerard Way**

With their debut album in the stores little more than nine months after their formation, My Chemical Romance were in an unusual position. Whereas most new bands would spend at least a couple of years zig-zagging across the country, building a following before scoring a record deal, by the summer of 2003 MCR had played relatively few shows outside of their home turf. While Alex Saavedra set about stirring up clouds of interest around the group by mailing pre-release copies of *I Brought You My Bullets, You Brought Me Your Love* to promoters, major record labels, DJ's and any band that might provide My Chem with a support slot in front of a potentially receptive audience, the band hit the road.

The first fruit of Saavedra's mail offensive became evident when 'Vampires Will Never Hurt You' became a surprise hit on college radio in Orange County, New Jersey. Seton Hall University's radio station, WSOU, established in 1978, had been one of the first US radio stations to find a regular scheduling slot for punk rock. A quarter of a century later, the station was equally quick to pick up on My Chem, when DJ Mario Comesanas became the first broadcaster to give the band airtime by playing 'Vampires'. 'The reaction was ridiculous – I knew that there was something special here,' recalled

*Gerard Way – dark architect of My Chem's unique sound and image.*

Comesanas. 'When we counted the requests there was so much more for them than there was for any other band at that time.'

'I heard "Vampires Will Never Hurt You", on a college radio station and it was probably the biggest thing to me in the world,' recounted Gerard during a 2005 interview with *Florida Entertainment Scene* website's Michael Montes. 'To this day, even hearing [*Three Cheers For Sweet*] *Revenge* songs on commercial radio isn't as big a deal as that first time hearing it on just a college radio station. I think it had like a hundred mile radius.'

As a succession of small stations picked up on My Chem, the pattern established with WSOU began to be repeated with increasing regularity – a DJ would spin 'Vampires' or 'Honey' and there'd be a near-instant influx of requests to hear more, or the same again. This incessant seepage onto the airwaves was bolstered by a relentless schedule of club dates. From the late summer of 2003 through to mid-April 2004, the quintet played dates from the southern states to Canada, supporting such groups as Massachusetts alt-rockers Piebald, Kentucky indie mainstays Elliott, and fast rising emo quintet Taking Back Sunday.

## 'We're a band with a lot of duality. We have a light side and a dark side and we just try to join the two.' – Gerard Way

For MCR, such a sudden burst of intense nationwide touring took some getting used to. Although Frank and Ray adapted to nightly performances fairly readily, Gerard found that he needed considerable Dutch courage in order to overcome persistent stage fright and general nerves. 'I was crazy all the time,' he told *NME*. 'I'd get the shakes if we were late to a show, because I had to start drinking immediately. There were times in the van where I'd pull a knife, just because I was excited.'

'I was so scared of performing that I had worked out the exact chemical combination to get me functioning in the band,' Gerard revealed in a 2005 *Spin* interview. 'I would drink from when I woke up until set time. I lived, breathed and shit for the show. I wore my stage clothes – the leather jacket, the boots – all the time.'

Because he was still mastering his chosen instrument, Mikey was often something of a static presence during shows, set back behind the intense mania of his brother's explosive stage performances and Ray's whirling dervish guitar heroics. The rookie bassist was also finding that constant gigging aggravated his phobias. 'There are times when big groups of people frighten me, and I have anxiety attacks if a lot of kids come up to me,' Mikey explained to *Rock Sound*. 'I have anxiety problems on stage because I'm still wet behind the ears . . . I used to drink heavily to get on stage because I had severe stage fright. I would drink with Gerard to the point where I felt at ease. He got mentally addicted to it, but I could do it recreationally.'

In February 2004, a welcome steadying influence manifested in the form of Brian Schechter. The young tour manager had first caught My Chemical Romance at their album launch gig the previous summer, and had followed the band closely ever since. 'I always listened to every demo the bands I used to tour with would get,' Schechter told concert information website *Pollstar*. 'I knew right when I heard it if there were a band I was going to stop touring and put everything into, it was My Chem.'

> 'It's rock'n'roll played by a bunch of man boys. We're hardcore R&B.' – Mikey Way

True to his word, Schechter gave up touring to manage MCR and launch his Riot Squad management company, with the Jersey quintet as the flagship artists. Having a full-time manager enabled the band to devote all their energies to performing and composing, as well as affording the group greater clout with the growing number of major labels that were showing interest.

One of Schechter's first moves was to set My Chem up with a tour alongside screamo heavyweights the Used. 'The tour gave me a great chance to see the drive and determination they had to be the band that they are,' observed Schechter. 'They've always had a very clear vision of who they wanted to be, so we were able to figure it out together.'

During the tour, Gerard struck up a friendship with Used frontman Bert McCracken and the duo quickly became inseparable, hard partying, minibar obliterating, drinking buddies. Although the nightly sessions did little for Gerard's liver, bonding with McCracken helped him get through the tour. The louche lifestyle also took its toll on Bert, who collapsed on stage during a 27 May show and was subsequently diagnosed as suffering from acute pancreatitis.

The tour also brought the rest of My Chem closer together, both as an increasingly effective gigging unit and as brothers in arms. 'You learn how to compromise with people, live with each other, and really take care of each other,' explained Frank. 'I know some bands that don't get along or don't have that kind of relationship or don't really know about each other and don't really hang out . . . I think that you learn most that you cherish that family. The most important thing is each other.'

In addition to providing MCR with an invaluable means of raising their vertically accelerating profile, the tour with the Used presented an opportunity for A&R personnel from many of the major labels to check them out. 'First, one major-label A&R guy came to our show,' Gerard told *Spin*'s Andy Greenwald. 'And then two, and then three and four. All of a sudden, it was like a weird fucking fungus all over the band!'

Over at Eyeball, both Marc Debiak and Alex Saavedra had realised that My Chem were becoming a phenomenon at a rate that outstripped the small label's ability to promote and support the band. By the summer of 2004, the group were being constantly courted by major labels and, with Eyeball not having the infrastructure to break the band nationally or internationally, it was clear that MCR had little option but to entertain the advances that were coming their way.

## 'People think that we're Brit-pop. That's kind of cool.' – Gerard Way

Aside from their growing following, one of the main reasons why so many major labels were getting the hots for the band was because A&R executives identified the group as part of the wave of emo groups, which they were fervently hoping would go some way to fill the sales void left by the collapse of the short lived nu-metal phenomenon.

The scramble to sign any outfit that was supposedly part of the emo sub-genre erupted in the wake of the success of Dashboard Confessional, whose angst-infused 2003 album *A Mark, A Mission, A Brand, A Scar* had crashed into the *Billboard* chart at Number 2. The hit album propelled frontman Chris Carrabba onto national TV and the covers of several magazines, sending major labels' marketing departments scurrying forth in search of the next Dashboard Confessional or Jimmy Eat World, whose 2001 album *Bleed American* had proved an unexpected, platinum-certified success.

Like nu-metal before it, the term 'emo' was often not to the liking of those bands tarred with that generic brush, and groups such as Jimmy Eat World sought to distance themselves. Originally coined as a means of distinguishing a sub-genre of straight-edge hardcore punk during the mid-1980s, the nomenclature was applied to all manner of bands and musical styles throughout the 1990s. It was almost as if the record industry – desperate for the kind of era-defining youth cults such as punk that simply don't exist anymore – were looking for a scene, any scene, to attach the label to.

*Bob Bryar – the final piece in the MCR jigsaw.*

Certainly, the emo tag was an ill-fitting straitjacket so far as My Chemical Romance were concerned. The band's extensive corpus of influences, and the manner in which they were applied during the recording of *I Brought You My Bullets . . .* were far too eclectic for one narrow sub-genre. Additionally, the idea of conforming to the strictures of a specific cult smacked of a certain kind of elitism that ran contrary to the band's inclusive ethos. 'What's different about us is that we are not really an emo band,' asserted Gerard in an interview for the *Punknews* website. 'We get booked on a lot of the same tours and shows with what people are calling emo bands. Everyone will obviously say that emo is a really loaded term, it is pretty much just what people are calling music that kids are playing nowadays.'

> 'When we first started we couldn't get booked on to shows as we were the opposite of everything that was emo – we've never really seen ourselves as that type of band.' – Gerard Way

'To me, "emo" is a piece of shit,' Mikey told *fasterlouder.com*'s kbro. 'It's like hair metal or one of those crappy sub genres within sub genres that will just fizzle out, it's a joke. Emo is really a genre of music within rock and roll, but to me emo means something different than what it has become . . . Emo to me is like Jimmy Eat World or Fallout Boy – it's rock music but a bit more emotive and intelligent.'

Many emo fundamentalists dismissed My Chemical Romance as too distinct from their own particular definition of the sub-genre. 'People made fun of us!' declared Mikey in an interview with Andy Greenwald for *Blender*. 'Emo was kids in recreation shirts and tight blue jeans, and we came out wearing makeup; we played hardcore shows at VFW halls, and Gerard dressed like Ziggy fucking Stardust. Everybody wanted to hate us. But we always had in our mind that we wanted to transcend this. We wanted to change the world.'

'I think we're more of a rock'n'roll band, but I think a lot of bands say that too,' Gerard told the *Chartattack* website's Pete Richards. 'I think if you look at bands even like International Noise Conspiracy, I think they would probably consider themselves a rock'n'roll band and they sound nothing like us. I think so many bands are just trying new sounds and new things and it's very hard to classify anyone anymore.'

Frank was also quick to distance himself from the nebulous emo scene. 'I think it's funny that there's this whole controversy over a word that no one really knows what it means anymore. I don't know what it is, but whatever it is, I just don't want to be it.'

'We're definitely closet Goths . . . some of us not so closet,' teased Gerard. 'We like all the macabre creepy stuff that Goths usually like, but we're more the variety that grew up reading comic books and watching horror movies as opposed to going to a club and dancing to Depeche Mode wearing fishnets. That's terrifying! We're not that kind of Goth, we're just kids who are obsessed with death.'

Regardless of My Chem's precise position in the sub-generic pantheon, it was undeniable that in order to progress they would have to leave Eyeball Records. In August 2003, they took the plunge into the big pond and signed with Warner/Reprise. 'It was hard,' admitted Alex Saavedra. 'It's sad when somebody says to you, "We don't want to work with you anymore, because we feel you can't do the job that you want." But it wasn't said meanly . . . it wasn't messy – it was like, "Okay dude – if that's the way it's gotta be then awesome – best of luck and I can't wait for the ride 'cos it's gonna be fun . . ."'

Although MCR had left Eyeball on something approaching the best of terms, the band realised that they would face the inevitable accusations of selling out, particularly from fans that viewed the group as their personal property and resented sharing them with a wider audience. Although the group would almost certainly make far more money on Reprise than would ever have been possible with Eyeball, it was hardly as if the change of label would be accompanied by a dilution of their beliefs or musical vision. Essentially an apolitical band, it is difficult to see how exactly My Chem could be identified as having sold-out. The idea of rock acts 'selling-out' has been around so long that it has become a brickbat thrown at any group that signs to a major. The accusation is now almost a kneejerk response – a tradition that runs from Dylan going electric, The Clash signing to CBS, through to Nirvana quitting Sub-Pop for Geffen.

> 'When we started this band we only hoped that people would actually want to come see us play.' – Gerard Way

Despite having no reason to be defensive about the move, Gerard was sensitive to such criticisms and broke the news to the MCRmy via the band's official website. 'This is an evolution and you can be part of the change or stuck eating your own shit on a quest for fire,' he wrote. 'Things are about to change for us . . . for all of us. From the kids who supported us at the start to those that are here now.

'We will always be an Eyeball Records band. The support, dedication, and love from that label got us where we are right now – and we did it as a family. I wanted to be the first to tell you before the gossip and the hearsay, I want to shout it from the street-lamps to the coils, in every fucked up slum, where every seedy club lives and breathes. We are coming to your town. We are taking back what's ours. We're all in this together . . . and by the way . . . we've signed to Reprise and we are fucking ready for the world to hear us scream.'

> 'You can't be in something unique and creative if you give a fuck what people say about you.' – Gerard Way

These were far more than the empty words of someone who'd just boarded the gravy train to bling central. The Reprise deal gave them unprecedented artistic control and freedom and subsequent events quickly demonstrated that no compromises were being made. In deed, as well as spirit, they remained an Eyeball band. 'They went back and took care of us, which was cool,' observed Marc Debiak.

With their debut album for Reprise already pencilled in for 2004, My Chem returned to touring on 27 September with an appearance at the annual Skatefest in Worcester, Massachusetts. Just over a week later the quintet embarked on a month-long tour with Murder By Death, A Static Lullaby and Vaux, which snaked across the northern states. The majority of these gigs were sold out and the trek was another successful exercise in expanding the MCR fanbase.

However, when the band returned home in November, all thoughts of tours, albums, major labels and new songs were swept aside by the death of Gerard and Mikey's grandmother, Elena – who had entered hospital to undergo what was scheduled as routine surgery. 'We didn't know what we were doing,' Gerard explained to *Kerrang!* 'We were afraid because we'd just signed to a major. We knew it was the right decision in our hearts; we were *hoping* we were ready. Then me and Mikey's grandma died, and it was pretty heavy, it was like, "Woah." We're in the middle of starting the real writing process and it was very difficult to get through.'

'It was really sad because I had just gotten off tour and she died the next day,' Gerard told *Alternative Press*. 'If you combined all the tours together and called it "the tour", I missed the last year and a half, practically, of this woman's life. And I get home, she dies the next day and I didn't get to see her. I was pretty devastated because she taught me how to sing and paint: basically everything I apply to this band, I got from her.'

*Mikey Way demonstrates his growing mastery of the bass at the KROQ Xmas Show, December 2004.*

In addition to being a huge personal blow to the Way brothers, Elena's death had a direct impact on the band – in addition to providing the funds for My Chem's first van, she had always been a reliable sounding board for Gerard's creative ideas. 'When we lost her, we lost this creative anchor,' he explained in an interview with *Wonka Vision*'s David Walter. 'You know, even though they were dark and violent, I would run past my grandmother the lyrics and drawings I worked on. She would offer me feedback and question why I was so angry and who was I so mad at, but she would also tell me she deeply enjoyed the poetry within the lyrics.'

Understandably, both brothers found their grandmother's death a traumatic and trying experience. Gerard, in particular, ran through a black spectrum of negative emotions as he attempted to come to terms with his loss. 'I wasn't with her when she died and it took me a while to get over that. I was very angry with myself,' he confessed to *Kerrang!* 'The emotions I went through at that moment completely fuelled *Revenge*. All the fucking anger, the spite, the beef with God, the angst, aggression and the fucking venom all came from that. When I lost her, I thought I was screwed. I was done. I had lost my mentor. That's why I took it so hard.'

> **'I'd really like to think that there's something else after death, I feel that there kind of has to be.' – Gerard Way**

So profound was Gerard's distress that instead of imparting some emotionally useful sense of closure, he found that the ceremonial aspects of Elena's burial only served to generate feelings of greater anger and deeper loss. 'At my grandmother's funeral I was really repulsed that she was treated as a sheep or something,' he told *NME*. 'I don't think they said her name once, they just talked about Jesus and stuff. I didn't think that was the point of why we were there that day. I didn't feel any comfort from the church.'

After attempting to sedate himself with the anxiety suppressant Xanax, Gerard had an eerie experience in a local shop that helped him begin to overcome his loss. 'I'm with my girlfriend at the grocery store picking up some stuff for Thanksgiving, which was the next day. It was really difficult to have a Thanksgiving because she'd just died and she'd always cooked for Thanksgiving, so we didn't even know if we were gonna have a holiday, but we figured we might as well go ahead,' he recalled in a 2004 interview for *Kerrang!* After taking a chicken pie from the freezer, he noticed his name spelt out in the frost that clung to the freezer cabinet's glass frontage. 'It was just the weirdest thing! I was freaked out at first and then really kinda moved. After that I was convinced it was a ghost because you couldn't even see any fingerprints. A ghost in the food aisle! But I felt a lot better after that.'

After Thanksgiving, Gerard and Mikey returned to the rehearsal studio to continue working up songs for the new album. However, Elena's death had left a profound impression on them both. 'Death is something we as a band faced head on,' Gerard told *The Sun*. 'When mine and Mikey's grandmother died, we began to look at death and the after-effects.' As he subsequently explained to *NME*, 'My love affair with death kind of came to an end when my grandmother died, and I realised [death] wasn't all it's cracked up to be.'

> 'The fans look out for each other. It's like a gang – but not in a negative way.' – Mikey Way

Although Gerard's creative anchor was no longer around, she would have a profound effect on the tone and content of My Chemical Romance's second album.

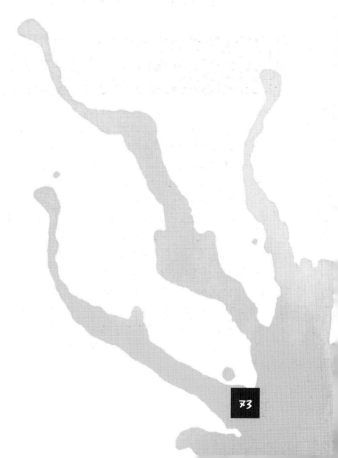

# Chapter 6

# NEVER COMING HOME

## 'We are all becoming what we want to become.' – Gerard Way

After a whistle-stop debut visit to the UK to play a short run of club shows, the opening months of 2004 saw My Chemical Romance withdraw from the sort of intensive touring that had dominated the previous year and a half, to concentrate on writing and recording their debut album for Reprise. To focus their creative energies, the band relocated to the heart of the US music industry. 'We actually drove to Los Angeles with all our stuff, and we lived in these apartments called the Oakwood Apartments,' Gerard told MTV's Chris Ward. 'Oakwood is basically home to child actors, out-of-work bands and porn stars. We saw a lot of child actors hanging out by the pool, constantly drinking. They were like fifteen years old, wasted and having these crazy Hollywood parties.'

'Realistically, I was into being in L.A. when we were writing,' observed Gerard in an interview with *Straight.com*'s Mike Usinger. 'I knew there would be a flavour to the record as a result of living in Los Angeles for two-and-a-half months. The phoniness and the sleaziness made a huge impact on me and the songs.'

Hardly surprisingly, one of the forthcoming album's themes would be mortality, generated by Gerard's reactions to his grandmother's recent death. 'It changed everything and

*Band of brothers – My Chem hang tough in February 2005.*

we were just about to finish writing the record,' he explained to the *Trouble Bunch Music* website's Jenna. 'So I re-evaluated what I was going to write lyrically. I didn't intend on it. I actually didn't even re-evaluate it, I just said, "Well, let me just write from the heart," and in the end, listening to the record, I was like, "Wow, this record is really about loss."'

**'Be yourself, don't take anyone's shit, and never let them take you alive.' – Gerard Way**

To produce the album, My Chem hired Howard Benson, a Drexel University engineering graduate who gravitated towards record production during the late 1980s, helming albums by heavy rock behemoths Motörhead, rapper Ice T's controversial metal project Body Count, and nu-metal God-botherers P.O.D. 'He had made four Motörhead records, and that's what got us interested about him and what also got us interested about him was the fact that he contacted us and that's how we like to work,' Gerard told *The Punk Site*'s Gary Hampton. 'I think a project is ultimately going to be better when you have people that mutually want to work together as opposed to having to convince a big shot producer to work *for* you. That was the case with him.'

Benson's sympathetic and supportive approach to record production proved ideal for MCR, who had distinct ideas about the sounds they wanted to produce but lacked the mixing desk mastery to realise them. 'It was awesome. He didn't want to mess with who we were at all,' Gerard enthused. 'He really taught us a great deal about song structure. He really was a coach. He didn't want to mess up the mould at all.'

In addition to the advantages inherent in working with a more experienced producer, My Chem also found that the greater resources available to major label bands benefited them significantly. 'Having a bigger budget gave us so many more tools at our disposal,' Frank explained to the *Life in a Bungalo* site. 'We had three weeks to write in L.A. before we actually started recording, and we had more time to be secluded and just get in each other's faces to really fine-tune the songs.'

'It was very cool,' Ray declared. 'When we recorded our first record we didn't have much time. The whole thing was recorded in about a week but for this one we actually had time to write.'

The downside of being newly signed to a major label was that, this time around, My Chemical Romance had a keenly felt obligation to fulfil Reprise's expectations. Furthermore, eighteen months of touring had increased the band's fanbase no end, and their growing army of followers were hungrily anticipating the follow up to *I Brought You My Bullets . . .* 'We knew there was going to be a lot of pressure because the first record kind of got a lot of critical attention but at the same time we realised that not many people had heard it,' recalled Gerard. 'We didn't let the pressure of making a good first record get to us and we also weren't super huge fans of a lot of the songs on that record and we knew what we could improve.'

'Heading back into the studio, we were anticipating it to be more difficult, so having a lot of ideas already prepared helped in the process,' Frank explained to Jeff Schechter of *AMP* magazine. 'As a band we wanted to capture the live aspects of our shows, because we didn't feel that the first record did our live performance the justice it deserves.'

Although the band had no shortage of ideas, when they arrived in Los Angeles they had insufficient songs to complete the album. Working up partially finished numbers into material that they could take into Magnolia Boulevard's Bay 7 Studios – which had previously hosted such diverse acts as the Smashing Pumpkins, 'Weird' Al Yankovic and Lisa Marie Presley – became the immediate priority. 'I think we had about half a record, then we got really inspired and ended up writing a whole bunch of songs, tweaking sections of songs we previously had and fragments became songs,' recalled Gerard. 'We had become so inspired we got finished with pre-production a week early.'

> **'If everybody just did one good thing for another person like a selfless good deed just think about how much better a place this would be.' – Frank Iero**

Under Benson's guidance, MCR recorded the thirteen songs that would make up *Three Cheers For Sweet Revenge* in around two months. 'I think we would have gotten it done a little faster than that but Howard wanted to kind of pace the record because we started moving so quickly,' revealed Gerard. 'He said, "Sometimes if you make a record too fast it gets away from you then when you're done with it you realise there's lots of stuff wrong with it." So, there were a lot of moments where [we] had to stop for a few days here and there.'

Opening with 'Helena', described by Gerard as 'an angry open letter to myself for being on the road so long and missing the last year of her life,' *Three Cheers . . .* thunders out of the starting block with angst-infused urgency. The song most directly influenced by the death of Gerard and Mikey's grandmother (Elena was sometimes known as 'Helen' to her friends), it also references a Misfits song of the same name – an altogether more visceral affair, which appeared on their post-Danzig 1999 album, *Famous Monsters*.

Kicking off with some frantic riffage and vocals, 'Helena' plunges through layers of pain and loss before hitting its soaring, bittersweet chorus. The track demonstrates how My Chem were continuing to experiment with their influences, combining musical DNA strings drawn from punk, pop-punk, heavy metal, rock and hardcore to create new and exciting hybrids.

'Helena' would subsequently be the third single taken from the album, hitting the *Billboard* Top 40 and making Number 20 in the UK, in addition to being voted 'Song of the Year' by *Spin* readers. 'I did have some sense it was going to be huge, but it almost had to be to honour a woman so amazing,' Gerard observed in an interview with *Spin*'s Kyle Anderson. 'When she died, I told her we would make a record so fucking loud that she would hear it all the way in heaven . . . or wherever it is you go. I was worried about it being huge because it was so personal – I didn't want to exploit my pain and her death.'

> **'Everyone wants something real, something that was created to invoke a positive feeling.' – Mikey Way**

Heralded by Mikey's thunderous bass intro, 'Give 'Em Hell, Kid' is a slice of blistering pop/punk that was described by Gerard as being about 'getting knocked the fuck up'. A lean, muscular anthem, the track is topped by an intense vocal performance that Howard Benson drew from the frontman. In order to free Gerard from any feelings of self-consciousness while he was laying down his vocals, the producer despatched his charge to the studio's attic. Aside from some headphones and a mic, Gerard was alone, in the dark, without any external stimuli. 'No one was allowed in there when I was doing my thing,' he told MTV. 'At first it was weird because I'm a showoff and I like people being able to watch me when I'm in the booth. But now, I can't imagine doing it any other way. I really let some intense stuff come out because I became very comfortable being naked and alone like that.'

A glorious exercise in applied melodrama, 'To The End' is a dual perspective dissection of the miserable rich inspired by William Faulkner's 1930 short story, *A Rose For Emily*. The track erupts into an uplifting chorus that immediately hooks the listener, and quick-

*Harmonic Generation – Gerard and Ray's twin vocal assault in full flow in Albany, New York, 2005.*

ly became established as a fan favourite. During the song's extended bridge section, Ray and Frank's guitar interplay demonstrates the genuine six-string synergy that was only in its very infancy when *I Brought You My Bullets . . .* was recorded. Like 'Give 'Em Hell, Kid', 'To The End' is performed with effective economy – a hallmark of Benson's insistence upon stripping any extraneous elements from the song structure. 'We made a real effort to kind of trim all the fat and get to the core of what makes a good song,' recalled Ray.

Featuring backing vocals from Bert McCracken, 'You Know What They Do To Guys Like Us In Prison' is a decadent yet upbeat exploration of life on the road, taking the idea of camaraderie into decidedly transgressive territory via references to kissing male friends and

> **'I think any world that was perfect would probably be destroyed very quickly.' – Gerard Way**

doing push-ups in drag. 'I draw on really weird sources, like comic books. I probably heard the line, "You know what they do to guys like us in prison," in a movie,' Gerard explained in an interview with Gene Stout for the *Seattle Post Intelligencer*. 'The song is sort of relevant to all the new bands coming out, with guys wearing women's pants and makeup and long hair. Music is evolving and it's sexy and it's getting dangerous again. And I like that. But if any of us went to jail, we'd have a really hard time.'

'Sometimes it feels like jail when you've got eight or nine guys in a van. It smells like jail – that's for sure,' Gerard told *Alternative Press*. 'Sometimes it feels like prison, but sometimes even the guys in prison, as fucked up and rough as it is, they buddy up and stick through it together. I think that's definitely one of the reasons I wanted Bert to sing on it, because he's one of the few people that I've met on the road and really connected with.'

Gerard subsequently identified the song as his favourite from *Three Cheers For Sweet Revenge*. 'I think it's very important for us as a band to write songs like "Prison" because it's kind of constantly breaking boundaries of what could be done by a modern rock band and still work. I think it's important to do those things and take risks.'

'We've always tried to switch the way people think about rock bands,' Gerard told *Blender*. 'That puts a dividing line between people. Are you on our side and you want to be different or are you on that side and you want to throw a football at my head?'

'I'm Not Okay (I Promise)' is another high octane number, which sees Gerard revisiting the theme of doomed romance. 'I like to think of it as a cry for help trapped in a

*New Jersey's finest – Frank Iero rocks the Warped Tour, August 2005.*

Three Cheers For Sweet Revenge – *the album that established My Chemical Romance as a unique rock phenomenon.*

pop song,' he explained. 'There was a girl I really liked, and she ended up taking really sleazy photographs with her boyfriend, and that really crushed me. I was just swimming in this pit of despair, jealousy and alcoholism. And when someone's in that situation, it's very rare that they turn to their mom or their best friend and say, "Hey, I'm not OK. I'm in really bad shape."'

The song features another bravura vocal performance from Gerard and is also enlivened by Ray's grandiose guitar heroics. 'I had talked to Gerard about this solo and we agreed that the song needed a huge guitar solo,' Ray revealed. 'Kind of a throwback to things like Zeppelin or Queen might do. You don't hear a lot of harmonised guitar solos nowadays or for that matter, guitar solos at all, so I wanted to make it as big as possible. I sat in that hotel room and recorded guitar after guitar until I finally found what I was looking for.' The track would later become the second single taken from the disc and made the British Top Twenty, as well as piercing the *Billboard* Hot 100.

After the runaway express train pace of *Revenge*'s opening five tracks, 'The Ghost Of You' provides momentary respite during its almost balladic opening verses, before the chorus kicks in and sends the number catapulting through a churning miasma of loss and regret. The single also features Israeli-born vocalist Rinat, who was formerly a member of the band Alone and subsequently signed to Black Eye records under her given name of Curious.

A pastoral organ segment courtesy of Benson segues 'The Ghost Of You' into 'The Jetset Life Is Gonna Kill You', a faster paced exploration of the hopelessness of addiction that refers largely to Gerard's own experiences. The song highlights MCR's musical development, with surefooted structural composition, subtle guitar elements during the opening verses and an explosive chorus reminiscent of Nirvana's tortured dynamism.

After the brief 'Interlude', comprising Gerard intoning the lyric, 'Saints protect her now/Come angels of the Lord, come angels of unknown,' over a sparse acoustic guitar backing, the album's second half charges in with the Iron Maiden-influenced axe attack of 'Thank You For The Venom'. Lyrically, the track deals with the absurd arrogance and presumptuousness of evangelism and contains the line, 'Sister, I'm not so much a poet, but a criminal' – a reference to 'Sister I'm A Poet', the b-side to Morrissey's 1988 single 'Everyday Is Like Sunday'. 'Morrissey is a huge influence on me, and I hope our songs are uplifting like his, even though the lyrics are pretty fucked up,' observed Gerard. 'There's nothing wrong with me specifically, but I do get depressed a lot. My therapist says I have a fear of success, but that's the beauty of this band. This is the first thing I've done that I haven't tried to sabotage. It has helped me overcome so many problems.'

Morrissey's influence on My Chem was underlined when 'Thank You For The Venom' was released as a single in Europe, and the group opted to include their live

> 'Me and Mikey, we are like a married couple. We share the same CDs and stuff.' – Gerard Way

cover version of his 1992 b-side 'Jack The Ripper'. Chronologically, 'Venom' was the first single lifted from *Revenge* and played a part in introducing the band to UK audiences, as it became MCR's first single to make the British chart, peaking at Number 71.

The concrete metaphor of a *faux* Ennio Morricone intro ushers in the sun-bleached, Western-themed 'Hang 'Em High', which draws much of its inspiration from the eponymous 1968 Clint Eastwood movie. 'Movies inspire me lyrically and they inspire me musically,' Gerard explained to *Designer* magazine editor Alex McCann. 'When we write a song we don't say lets make it a real punk rock song, we say let's make a cowboy song or a cabaret song so when the song first starts it will sound like a cabaret tune from one of the shows.'

The track breaks all safety limits for raw excitement, and features guest vocals from former Black Flag and Circle Jerks frontman Keith Morris – who had contacted MCR to say how much of a fan he was. 'Black Flag are my favourite band of all time. "Nervous Breakdown" is probably the best punk rock song of all time and Keith Morris is one of my all time heroes,' enthused Frank. 'Keith Morris actually sang on *Three Cheers For Sweet Revenge* and I got to eat Chinese food with him and talk for a little while. That wasn't a bad moment.'

A pounding dissection of death and revenge, 'It's Not A Fashion Statement, It's A Deathwish' sees Gerard drawing upon the comic book section of his library of pop cultural influences. The song features the lyric, 'You get what everyone else gets – you get a lifetime,' which owes its provenance to the character Death from Neil Gaiman's award-winning DC/Vertigo series *The Sandman*. Published between 1988 and 1996, the series featured the saga of the Lord of Dreams and was among the most literate works ever presented in the four-colour medium, becoming the only comic book ever to win the World Fantasy Award and spawning a host of spin-offs. (In 2006 Dancing Ferret Records released *Where's Neil When You Need Him?*, a seventeen-track tribute album to Gaiman, spearheaded by a contribution from eccentric singer-songwriter Tori Amos. The album's booklet featured a foreword written by Gerard.)

> 'It's important to me, to us, that our audience knows that they don't have to act in that stupid way that some rock bands want them to.' – Gerard Way

Kicking off with a subtle opening verse that brings to mind the Cure, 'Cemetery Drive' bursts into soaring life to reveal itself as a heartfelt evocation of the loss engendered by the suicide of a loved one or friend. 'We are a very anti-suicide band because we have been dealing with mental depression all our lives, and I mean everyone gets depressed but so few people in music address depression,' Gerard explained to *Crush Media*'s Jason Schleweis and Rob Todd. 'And that's always just been one of our messages because so few people address what's wrong with them and communicate their problems.'

In as much as it is possible for any rock band, My Chem have always attempted to engage actively and positively with their audience over the issues of suicide and self-harm. 'We really want to get that across to people that there is always someone to talk to – even us,' asserted Gerard. 'Especially us if you are at a show and you are feeling upset. I mean I have had tons of people come up and talk to me about it and that's the best. When we can talk about that, rather than my hair or some shit like that.'

*Three Cheers For Sweet Revenge* reaches its conclusion with 'I Never Told You What I

*Have afro, will rock – Ray Toro's accomplished guitar technique has drawn comparisons with Queen's poodle-haired axe-god Brian May.*

Do For A Living', a churning, metal-tinged finale to the fragmented tale of the vengeful lover that features as an intermittent motif throughout the album. 'It always felt to us like this band is about fulfilling a destiny,' Gerard observed. 'And the story of the record is linked to that. There's this guy who's doing very much what he feels he should be doing, and if he has to kill 1,000 evil men to get to the woman he loves, then he'll do it. And there's a lot of sacrifices we make as well.'

> **'We're not a joke band by any stretch of the imagination, but you can't take yourself too seriously.' – Gerard Way**

'It really doesn't follow a linear thing,' Gerard explained to *Cincinnati City Beat*'s Alan Sculley. 'It's more like you're getting little snippets of the story, which at the end should make up the whole part.'

The proof that My Chem's move to a major label was justified is clearly evident within *Three Cheers For Sweet Revenge*. 'We were a bit apprehensive, waiting to see how the label treated us in the studio,' Frank admitted. 'But it worked out great, Reprise gave us creative licence to create the sort of record we wanted, this is definitely the record we set out to make.'

Described by Gerard as 'A big obnoxious sounding rock record', the album is an evident progression on its predecessor, both musically and in terms of the lyrics. 'What we really learned during this record was that whenever we experimented and tried something a little different, the songs worked really well,' Gerard told *Straight.com*'s Mike Usinger. 'In the future, I can see us moving even more into a rock-type realm, with lots more melody and an overall largeness. And I can see us getting even darker as far as subject matter goes.

'I felt like it was very successful. There are some very subversive things in there lyrically and a lot of stuff that comes in under the radar,' asserted Gerard. 'The band and I think the new record is better. It's a band that's grown and evolved, when we made the first record we were only a band for three months. From touring we became the band we are now and that's reflected onto the album.'

Creatively, *Revenge* hits all its targets, referencing the full widescreen scope of MCR's musical and pop cultural influences, while producing a body of work that holds together in a unified manner. 'We can't really write songs that sound alike,' Gerard told the *Trouble Bunch Music* website. 'We like to capture moods and you can definitely pinpoint those moods. You can say this is the same kind of mood or feel. We like to explore themes and moods but style is something we can't live with ourselves doing over and over. And if that means we run out of material eventually then that's fine because you'll never get something twice from us.'

The diversity of material within the album also released the band from the emo ghetto. 'We took a lot of risks on this record because we knew we had been put into the genre of emo because of the tours we were doing,' Gerard told MTV's Jon Wiederhorn. 'We always felt we were much more of a rock and roll band. So that's what we really tried to assert this time.

'There was this feeling of bringing a real rock band back. Even when you see us live it sounds as if there's ten guitarists up on stage 'cos Frank and Ray have so much going on and complement each other so well,' enthused Gerard. 'We think very much about in terms of what it's going to be like live when we play. There are songs that we flat out wouldn't put on a record if we couldn't play them live.'

**'We're as street as fuck.' – Gerard Way**

In addition to plotting the band's lyrical and thematic direction, Gerard also brought his illustrative talents to bear on the album's sleeve art. 'Coming up with the ideas and a visual aesthetic for the band is the fun part, it's the easy part, but executing it with that kind of thing is very hard because I find it difficult to kind of remove myself from it, I'm too close to the project. When I draw something, I'd rather have somebody else do it, but with this one the people at Warner loved it so much they convinced me to use it.'

Once the album was released, a delighted Gerard declared himself more than satisfied with the way that the entire process had turned out. 'It feels amazing,' he told *Crush Media* magazine. 'We had to work three times the amount as a major label band just to get out there. It's really hard, but it's a really big victory to have that record in stores everywhere, too walk in and see it . . . and the response we have been getting is just incredible. The day before the record dropped it just felt like Christmas and now it feels like a party everyday.'

With the album entering the *Billboard* chart at Number 28 and the band set to join the high-profile Warped tour for a run of shows to support it, it was obvious to all that the band had moved up several levels. 'This new record is really gonna blow up,' declared Frank. 'It is just as true to what was done with *Bullets* but more energetic and over the top. I can't wait for the fans to get their hands on the new record. We are set up to tour so much in the next year; I forget what my house looks like already.'

# Chapter 7

# FEELING NUMB

**'We don't want to be rich, we just want to try and reach as many people as possible. And really try to make a difference.'**
**– Gerard Way**

On 9 June 2004, the day after *Three Cheers For Sweet Revenge* hit the stores, My Chemical Romance set out on a short run of bar and club shows with Canadian rockers Boys Night Out and New York indie quartet Nightmare Of You. These eight dates were little more than the touring equivalent of an *hors d'oeuvre*, ahead of almost eighteen months of solid gigging that would see the group blaze their way across the US, UK, Europe and Japan.

The first major step on what would prove to be a very long march indeed was My Chem's debut on the Vans Warped Tour, which set out on 25 June. Established in 1995, the tour combines live music with extreme sports and takes its name from the now defunct *Warp* magazine, which featured skateboarding and surfing features alongside its rock'n'roll coverage. Sponsored since its inception by footwear manufacturer Vans, the tour built a reputation for low ticket prices and high excitement, being in many ways the louder, snottier little brother to Jane's Addiction frontman Perry Farrell's increasingly staid Lollapalooza event. 'Lollapalooza always has the same type of bands like Sonic Youth or the Pixies, bands that I love and I'll go see, but kids are unaware of what that music means,' observed Gerard. 'But [the] Warped Tour has always been

*Release the bat – Gerard commands the Mean Fiddler stage*
*at one of the band's first London gigs, September 2004.*

based around like youth culture and youth music, like what youth is listening to at the time. And since that's what it represents, I can't imagine it going stale.'

The 2004 tour got off to a soggy start when the opening show in Houston was postponed due to torrential rain. 'It was like a snow day vibe,' recalled Gerard. 'Then the rain let up, so everyone was hanging out in the parking lot drinking. I think it was a great way to start the tour because everyone got to meet each other and old friends met up again. I got to see guys I hadn't seen in a year because we tour so much. It was like a family reunion.'

My Chem were scheduled to appear throughout the first half of the Warped Tour's two-month run, starting with the abandoned Houston show and ending in Chicago on 24 July. For Frank,

> 'I have the potential to be a fantastic alcoholic.' – Gerard Way

playing the tour was the fulfilment of a long held ambition. 'Ever since I was in bands at thirteen, I tried to do battle of the bands, play Warped Tour and things like that. I never actually won any of the battle of the bands but it's a dream come true to be on Warped . . . it's unlike any other tour we've been on and you can't prepare for it in any way. But it's definitely a dream come true to play with some of my favourite bands of all time.'

In addition to MCR, the line-up also featured such acts as punk stalwarts Bad Religion and the Vandals, Lars Frederiksen and the Bastards, (Rancid guitarist Frederiksen's side project), actress Juliette Lewis's rock project Juliette and the Licks, and My Chem's long-time homeboys Thursday. 'I got to see my favourite bands every day, and they treated us like peers – that was an amazing experience,' enthused Frank. 'The Warped Tour kids are unlike any other kids. You don't feel like you are playing a show, you feel like a travelling carny . . . We're a young band, and bands like the Bouncing Souls and Alkaline Trio took us under their wing. To be validated by these staples of punk rock is just amazing.'

Certainly, Alkaline Trio frontman and guitarist Matt Skiba liked what he saw in the Warped debutants. 'I wandered out into the crowd, [MCR] started playing, and I got kind of the same feeling that I got going to Naked Raygun shows. They were so good and sounded so great, and the energy exchange with the crowd was something that I hadn't seen in a long time. I had no choice. I had to start dancing. My drink was full when I walked in there, and five seconds later, it was all over a bunch of kids' heads.'

Although My Chemical Romance enjoyed hanging out with the other bands on the tour, the run of open-air shows was a period of adjustment for the quintet. 'We're not a festival band,' Gerard declared. 'Festivals are something completely alien to us. They always have been. So getting on stage the first time at Warped was really terrifying for us.'

Additionally, Gerard was also coming to terms with performing the emotionally laden songs that comprised *Three Cheers For Sweet Revenge*. 'In the beginning was difficult, then it became a release and now it's like a remembrance,' Gerard told *Convertlivewire*'s Phil Bonyata and Karen Bondowski in 2005. 'I'm not working out my issues anymore with these things but I'm remembering them and I feel the emotion mainly during the choruses especially. Those things were designed by us to hit you right in the heart. It hit us in the heart and that's what those songs do.'

Many of the Warped Tour bands got together at the end of each show for a huge nightly barbecue. This, along with the many hours spent waiting for their scheduled performance slot to come around, meant that there was almost unlimited licence for bands to party hard and drink heavily. For Gerard, the boozy carnival atmosphere on the tour exacerbated his growing dependence on alcohol and prescription downers. 'I worked out a system where if we played at noon, I was basically just hung over, still drunk probably from the night before. If we were playing at one or two, I was already drunk,' he confessed to Scot Heisel of *Alternative Press*. 'If [I wasn't] fully drunk, then I was trying to get drunk at any signings we had to do. After that, I would continue to get drunk well until the [day's tour stop] was done, until bus call. Bus call would come, or sometimes before it, and I would pop a bunch of Xanax and basically be cracked out.'

> **'I don't understand the "cutesy frontman" tag I've been given. I just thought people liked me because I'm a crazy asshole.' – Gerard Way**

'What sent Gerard over the edge was after we finished recording,' Frank told *Kerrang!* 'He had recorded certain songs as though he was playing a character. In order to play those characters he had to get fucked up, which meant that, live, he felt he needed to be in the same headspace. That led to him drinking a lot.'

'Things started to spiral out of control,' Gerard explained to *Straight.com*'s Mike Usinger. 'I've always had a problem with drinking and mixing alcohol with pills, and it started to get the best of me. So the same way I was functioning just to sing when we were doing the record, I functioned just to play the shows when we did Warped. By the end of tour, what I was doing to myself was affecting my performances, my appearance, and my energy.'

Immediately after MCR's run on the Warped Tour, the band continued on the road with a series of dates with the likes of Less Than Jake, Funeral For A Friend and the Lostprophets. By now, Gerard was consuming unrestrained quantities of sedative pills, washed down with at least a bottle of vodka every day. With some inevitability, during a show at the Belvedere Festival Park in Louisville, Kentucky, he finally came unglued. 'They handed me a cordless mic, so I decided I was gonna make a big joke out of it,' he told *Revolver*. 'I climbed all around the stage. I didn't even know where I was half the set. And I ended the show on the second stage while my band was on the first stage.'

Gerard's drunken capering infuriated Frank, who didn't speak to his bandmate for the next two days. 'I was so fucking mad. Geoff Rickly and Daryl Palumbo saw him under the stage and they're telling him where to run to next. And after the gig, Daryl was laughing, and Geoff's like, "Wow, you guys just fall apart real well, don't you?"'

Despite egging Gerard on during his unscheduled walkabout, Rickly was sympathetic to the frontman's condition. 'It's weird to say, because they're a band and they can do what they want – but those are our friends. You don't want to see them get sucked into something you've had your band sucked into.'

Funeral For A Friend drummer Ryan Richards had observed Gerard demolish bottles of vodka backstage, and was struck by the way in which his alcohol-infused performances became vicariously compelling. 'He would start drinking well before going onstage. The more he drank the more unhinged the show would be. It was like watching a car crash. You couldn't take your eyes off him. Everyone was talking about him, about the band with the crazy frontman.'

Despite the numbing effect of his pills and booze regime, Gerard was aware of the downward spiral he had locked into. 'I thought that was the way I was going to end, the way I was going to create something beautiful was to completely go to oblivion,' he told *NME*. 'I mean, that's like the ultimate artist's fantasy, that you're going to make a statement by destroying yourself, you know, and so I was extremely self-destructive . . . because it's the oblivion you're allured by.'

At the beginning of August 2004, MCR travelled to Japan for a short run of festival appearances. Unknown to the rest of the band, a couple of nights before they were due to fly out, Gerard had hit crisis point after getting completely wasted on a cocktail of booze and cocaine at a Killers gig. 'Nobody in my band knew,' he recalled. 'I had a really good way of hiding stuff.'

The following morning Gerard awoke, feeling dehydrated, depressed and more anxious than ever. 'I never felt more suicidal. I woke up at five in the morning and nobody was awake. I was strung out, hung over and really desperate. I had tons of pills on me and lots of liquor. I thought [killing myself] would be so easy.' Instead, he phoned Brian Schechter, who spent the best part of the next three hours talking him down.

Although Gerard joked that he was terrified to tour Japan, 'because we are positive we'll lose Ray and he'll never come home. The boy has a passion for Asian women that is only rivalled by his love for He-Man action figures,' the frontman was privately dreading the tour because of his unstable physical and psychological condition. 'I was terrified,' he admitted. 'All I did was sweat two days before Japan. I sweat buckets, drank and loaded up on my pills for the trip.'

Once there, Gerard spent the majority of his time in Japan getting drunk and taking Xanax to numb his feelings of desperation and hopelessness. After a gig in Osaka where he'd spent much of the gig *under* the stage, he became seriously ill – doubled up, vomiting uncontrollably, and unable to cope with his body's rebellion against the incessant abuse it had absorbed. 'Ray turned to our manager while I was vomiting and said, "You've got to get this dude some help. He's sick, look at him." By sick, he didn't mean I was ill either. He meant sick like I wasn't going to make it. He was right. I knew I had to stop.'

> 'Any time you mix drinking with narcotics, something bad can happen.' – Frank Iero

'It was a vicious circle,' Gerard later admitted to *Blender*. 'I needed it to function but it made me want to kill myself. It made me extremely unpredictable and dangerous to myself. I didn't want it to get to the point where it became like a VH1 *Behind the Music* where they show this really bad picture of me 30 pounds overweight, throwing up on the floor in Berlin. I didn't want that to happen to this band.'

After experiencing withdrawal during the long flight back to the US, Gerard said an emotional goodbye to his bandmates and checked in to see his therapist. 'He said, "When you leave here, you're going to go buy Brian Eno's *Music For Airports*, and it's gonna calm you the fuck down,"' Gerard recalled in an interview with *Entertainment Weekly*'s Whitney Pastorek. 'I had a bottle of vodka in the trunk just in case, and I listened to [the album] in a parking lot and felt a lot better. So I threw the bottle out and went to AA.'

In his hour of need, Gerard turned to his bandmates for support and understanding. 'I came to them and said, "Look, I have a problem, and I think it's been affecting the band,"' he told MTV. 'It was becoming a normal thing for me to drink before the show. And it was something I was very defensive about. But they were really supportive.'

'We knew he drank too much,' explained Ray. 'I don't think we realised the full extent of the problem, though. We felt like, "What did we miss? Could we have done something sooner?" But I don't think Gerard would have listened if we had, I think he had to do it for himself.'

'Gerard needs protecting too,' insisted Mikey in an interview for *Metal Hammer*. 'If you look through history, most of the people that died tragically or imploded or went crazy were the headman of the band. It's not a coincidence, it's obvious that they didn't have enough support around them.'

'I needed that support,' declared Gerard. 'I'm still scared, though. I worry it could happen again and I could end up dead. When this band started, it saved my life. I got saved, then I went off the rails again and the band came to my rescue a second time. I hope it's now an excuse to keep stable, because it's all that I have now.'

## 'I know the minute I touch a drink again is the minute I lose everything that I've got.' – Gerard Way

Much of Gerard's excessive use of alcohol and prescription drugs was an attempt to keep a lid on his anxieties. His dependencies increased in tandem with the emotional and psychological duress he was subject to. The fact that he reached a crisis point during the Japan tour was hardly surprising – it was a journey that he was reluctant to make, partly because he feared that his unstable condition might cause the band to implode. A secondary cause for concern about My Chem's future was provided by Matt, whose lack of technical ability had been apparent since the recording of *I Brought You My Bullets . . .*, and who had recently become increasingly distant from his bandmates.

After a good deal of discussion between Gerard, Ray, Frank, Mikey and Brian Schechter, it was decided to dismiss Matt after the gigs in Japan. 'The main reason was that we weren't having fun being in the band,' explained Ray, who along with Schechter went to visit Matt in order to break the news to him. 'He had to have known in his heart – whether he'll admit or not – that he wasn't performing up to the way we needed to perform. You had to have been fucking blind to not see the relationship problems between each of us and him – that we just didn't get along.'

The band chose not to make a statement concerning Matt's sacking because, as Ray explained: 'We didn't want to get into a pissing match, and we didn't want to have this sort of he-said, she-said bullshit.' Perhaps not surprisingly, Matt found the decision difficult to stomach. 'Do I think I've been shafted? Yeah,' he asserted in *Kerrang!* 'What happened to the five brothers that loved each other more than anything else on Earth? I gave up everything for each of them.'

Refusing to be sucked into a highly public dispute, Gerard issued a generalised response: 'If I'm going to say anything about anyone being fired, then it's that this band is about giving a shit about each other, about looking people in the fucking eye and knowing you care about them, that they care about you and

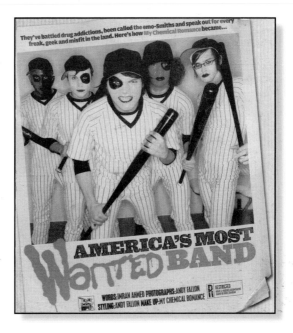

They've battled drug addictions, been called the emo-Smiths and speak out for every freak, geek and misfit in the land. Here's how My Chemical Romance became...

AMERICA'S MOST Wanted BAND

WORDS:IMRAN AHMED PHOTOGRAPHS:ANDY FALLON STYLING:ANDY FALLON MAKE UP:MY CHEMICAL ROMANCE

knowing that's the truth. That's not directed at Matt, that's directed at the whole band.'

Fortunately for My Chem, a replacement for Pelessier was close at hand. Bob Bryar had got to know the band through touring with MCR in his capacity as front-of-house sound technician for the Used. After the two bands went their separate ways, Bob maintained his friendship with MCR and sometimes hung out with the group while they were on the road. 'I kind of noticed that the other drummer didn't get along with anybody,' Bob told *Zero* magazine. 'The mood of the band was horrible. They weren't like a real band who enjoys being on stage together or doing anything together. After a show he would go off on his own. Not to talk shit or anything but he was kind of an asshole. We started talking like, "Man I wish you played drums in our band."'

'I was kind of depressed because I wasn't doing what I wanted to do,' Bryar recalled in an interview with *Modern Drummer*'s Waleed Rashidi. 'I was watching other drummers live out their dreams and play drums every night. Meanwhile, I was the guy behind the board making their drums sound good.'

With the key to Bob's ambitions dovetailing with My Chem's lack of a drummer, the timing of the band's call couldn't have been more opportune. 'They asked me if I wanted to play drums and I said "yes," but they hadn't really heard me play drums before,' he revealed in an interview with *Rhythm* magazine. 'I was out with the Used, we were doing a tour called the Projekt Revolution Tour and I left in the middle of that. I went to New Jersey and we had one day when we practised together. The next day we flew out to shoot the "I'm Not Okay" video and two days after that we went out on tour.'

'It was a huge leap of faith for us to call up Bob, but it was the best thing we could have done,' Frank revealed. 'He came to practice and played really well, and then we went on tour right away. Four shows in, we were like, "Get the fuck out of here! This is amazing!" We were so much tighter and we were all smiling while we were playing.'

'I think he joined at the scariest time in the band,' Gerard told *Kerrang!* 'A lot of people would have wanted to stay away, because no one knew what was going to happen. We hadn't even shot a video yet. A lot of people banked on us failing.'

Unlike his new bandmates, Bob had no ties to New Jersey. Born in Chicago on New Year's Eve 1979, the future MCR drummer grew up in the pleasant suburb of Downers Grove. A dexterous child 'who took apart radios and stuff and then tried to put them back together and realised they didn't work', Bob started experimenting with drumming when he was just four years old.

## 'I'm not psychotic . . . I just like psychotic things.' – Gerard Way

As a youngster, Bob made the five-mile, trip south to attend Eisenhower Junior High School where he received his first musical training, playing drums in jazz bands and orchestral ensembles. He continued to play in a number of formal and informal groups throughout his teenage years, during which he attended Downers Grove South High School. 'I was really into playing jazz and orchestral percussion,' Bob recalled. 'I was going to go to school to study orchestral percussion, but I thought about it and it didn't seem like something I could do for the long run and still feel happy with it. So I started to join bands and play rock music.'

Bob's main influences were jazz fusion heavyweight Dave Weckl and Rush drummer/lyricist Neil 'the Professor' Peart. The high levels of technical accomplishment demonstrated by Weckl and Peart combined with Bob's natural aptitude to create a style that was sometimes a little too baroque for straight-up, no-nonsense rock'n'roll. 'I'd tend to overplay,' he admitted. 'This kind of music isn't about everybody playing as much as they can. It's about feeling from listening to it. And that's one thing I learned very quickly.'

Having set about modifying his style to suit the rock canon, Bob found it difficult to find a band that would match his immediate dedication, that breathed, ate and slept rock'n'roll. 'The only way I was going to play drums was by joining a band that was focused on succeeding,' he explained to *Rock Sound.*

Discouraged by his inability to find anyone with similarly intense ambitions, Bob relocated to Gainesville, where he gained a degree in recording engineering from the University of Florida. During this period, Bob took a job at Disney World in order to help with the bills. 'I thought I was going to do something cool, but when I went to my initiation day and opened up the packet it said I was working on *The Little Mermaid* theme show. I was so pissed. My first costume was white pants, a blue and white striped shirt and a sailor hat. Later I played drums for the *Aladdin* stage show. I finally quit because they yelled at me about my sideburns.'

'Japan is amazing. It's like a whole country inside a mall. Everything there rules.' – Frank Iero

After graduating, Bob scored a job as the house sound man at the House of Blues concert hall in Chicago, where he worked for around two years. Still keen to get a group off the ground, Bob decided to go on the road as a sound engineer and drum technician. From this, he graduated to tour managing for various bands such as the Used. 'I just moved up the ladder, to the point where I was doing really well in that field. I had no problem getting work, and I was making good money,' he recalled. 'But I'd still watch the drummer, and I'd be like, I want to be playing drums. It was so frustrating, because in between the sound check and the show, I'd stand and play on a practice pad in the corner.'

When he received the call to try out for the vacant drum stool in My Chemical Romance, Bob didn't hesitate, quitting his job the following day. 'I would have done it even if you would have told me, "You guys will be playing to 100 people every night for the rest of your career," because that's how much I like the band and how much I wanted to play the drums.'

With a video shoot and tours imminently looming, it would have been catastrophic had Bob not meshed with the band. Fortunately, with both parties knowing one another pretty well and Bob's drumming abilities proving more than adequate, My Chem were back up to full strength just days before they were due to head out on the road. 'If there is a God,' declared Frank, 'I thank him everyday for bringing us Bob.'

# Chapter 8

# HERE'S ONE FOR ALL THE MISFITS. . .

**'Journalists usually portray us as a fucked-up, dark, vampire, alcoholic rock band. Until they meet us.'**
**– Gerard Way**

The hectic pace at which My Chemical Romance had to recruit a new drummer, shoot the video for 'I'm Not Okay (I Promise)', and then head out on the road meant that the impact made by *Three Cheers For Sweet Revenge* initially passed them by. The album was met by generally positive reviews in the major music press. In his three-star write-up, *Rolling Stone*'s Kirk Miller praised the band's 'sneaky sense of humour' and Gerard's 'endearing warble', before declaring the disc 'a hell of a good time'. Over at *Blender*, Andy Greenwald focused on the band's youth appeal, observing that *Revenge* was 'perfect for pissing off your parents, carving into your binder or auditioning for summer-stock *Phantom of the Opera*'.

For a major label debut by a still relatively new band, *Revenge* made a more than respectable dent on the US chart, cracking the Top 30 and topping *Billboard*'s 'Top Heatseekers' list for new and developing artists. Additionally, the album also achieved moderate chart success in the UK, Australia and New Zealand. Given that it had largely been promoted through incessant touring and word of mouth, this represented a significant achievement for a band that, less than two years earlier, had been pleased to draw an audience that reached three figures.

*An army of five – My Chem's adoption of band*
*uniforms highlighted the group's collective unity.*

The absence of any promotional videos in advance of *Revenge*'s release meant that the band's steady rise was driven by their grass-roots support and an online buzz from their own website and MySpace page. In order to reach a wider audience, it was imperative to capture the attention of those unable to get to gigs, who took their fix of new bands direct from MTV.

In mid-August 2004, the band shot their first fully professional video under the aegis of Marc Webb, an up-and-coming director who was establishing a reputation through his work with such diverse acts as Green Day, Maroon 5 and the Backstreet Boys.

A well-observed pastiche of the trailers for rights-of-passage comedies such as Wes Anderson's 1998 movie *Rushmore*, the 'I'm Not Okay' promo also satirises Gerard, Mikey, Frank and Ray's teenage experiences of being marginalised. Packed with visual gags and subtly incisive satire, the band are portrayed as quirky, croquet-playing, Salbutamol-huffing nerds harassed by the usual high-school jocks. The concept was suggested by Webb and found immediate favour with the band. 'He came up with the idea of having a movie that didn't exist, and have a trailer for that movie,' explained Gerard. 'I hear a lot of people who had never heard of the band at first watch it and they think it's from an actual movie.'

> **'We're very honest about who we are. On stage we're something very extraordinary and offstage we're very ordinary.' – Gerard Way**

Although Bob appears fleetingly in the video, he is largely obscured by Gerard and his name is omitted from the *faux* movie credits toward the clip's end. At this point, it was not completely certain whether he would become a permanent member of the group. However, once he had played his first few gigs, any thoughts of a trial period became unnecessary. 'Bob is really hard to describe,' mused Gerard in an interview for *Zero* magazine. 'He's kind of like the mystery man. There's a lot of things we don't know about Bob, but what we do know about him is that he's a really good dude, he makes us laugh. We think of him as a brother.'

The single of 'I'm Not Okay (I Promise)' was not released for another four months, whereupon it hit the Top Twenty in Britain and achieved a more modest Number 86 placing in the USA.

After a high profile appearance at the Warped Tour Tenth Anniversary concert along-

*We are the kids your parents warned you about –*
*My Chem ham it up for the cameras Manson-style.*

side Rancid, Less Than Jake, Andrew WK and the Vandals, MCR joined up with the Nintendo Fusion tour. Sponsored by the Japanese video games giant as a means of promoting their latest products, as well as showcasing emerging talent, the tour was a relatively new addition to the summer calendar, having only been inaugurated the previous year. In addition to offering My Chem a run of around 30 shows alongside labelmates Story Of The Year, Welsh rockers the Lostprophets and Florida quintet Anberlin, Gerard and company were delighted to get their hands on some free swag in the form of consoles and games. 'The first day they gave us a Gamecube with four wireless controllers and *Mario Kart*, which was really nice of them and we play that stuff all the time,' enthused the frontman. 'They just recently gave us *Donkey Konga*, the bongo game, they gave us four sets of bongos so we're very excited, they're so nice to us, you know? It definitely has its benefits.'

**'We put everything we have into every show.' – Bob Bryar**

After completing their run on the Fusion Tour on 26 October 2004, MCR continued gigging alongside Story Of The Year throughout the following month. On 13 November, the band found themselves on one side of a stand-off against some over-zealous Californian police, during a special show organised by Los Angeles radio station KROQ-FM. Alongside all-girl bubblegum rockers the Donnas, My Chem were scheduled to attend a signing session and then play a set in the car park of the Orange, CA branch of electrical retailers Best Buy. However, the organisers had grossly underestimated the likely attendance and when a crowd of around 3,000 turned up, many of whom were keen to meet the bands and have albums and KROQ calendars signed, a nervous local police sergeant insisted that the signing session be curtailed.

Unhappy at disappointing *anyone* who'd taken the trouble to turn out for his band, Gerard offered to meet everybody 'even if it took all night'. When the frontman took the stage, he announced that My Chem would meet up with everybody after their set. 'The music was cranking, and there was a lot of activity in the crowd, trying to start a mosh pit and that just made the audience more excited,' opined OPD Officer Dave Hill. 'So much so that the Sergeant was close to preparing to shut down the show.'

However, once the performance was underway, it appeared as if the police were looking for an excuse to bring the event to an early end. 'Halfway through our set, our manager started motioning for me to come over to the side of the stage. I thought something really bad had happened,' Gerard told MTV's James Montgomery. 'I went over to him, and he said, "You have to stop cursing, or we're going to get in a lot of trouble, maybe even arrested. Or they're going to try to shut the show down.'"

Despite the constabulary's scandalised reaction to what they later described as 'Not just profanity, but vulgarity,' the remainder of MCR's set passed off without incident. After the show, Gerard and the band attempted to make good on their promise of

> **'We've never been to China. We've never been to South America. There's a lot of places My Chemical Romance hasn't played a show yet.' – Ray Toro**

meeting those who'd come out to support them, but were prevented from doing so by the OPD, who insisted that the lot be cleared by 5pm – when the city-approved permit expired. 'It took fifteen security guards to get all the fans to leave the parking lot,' explained Gerard. 'It was probably the biggest bum-out of our career.'

Disappointed by the police's intractable insistence on applying the letter of the law, the band issued a press statement apologising to all those who'd been let down. 'If we would have stayed we were told we would have been arrested – which is really no big deal. But we realised that would have solved nothing. It wouldn't have changed the fact that the majority of you would walk away without us getting to meet you and at that point would have just been a show of bravado or arrogance. This was not KROQ's fault – in fact, they tried as hard as they could to make it so we could stay all night and sign. Nor was it Best Buy's fault. It really wasn't anyone's fault. The police wanted us out of there and there was nothing to be done about it.'

Apart from a short break over the holiday season, there was little let-up in the band's relentless tour schedule as 2004 gave way to 2005. With their profile rising on an almost daily basis, the quintet received some mainstream television exposure with two appearances on *Late Night with Conan O'Brien* either side of Christmas, and a typically energetic performance of 'I'm Not Okay' on a January edition of *Late Night with David Letterman,* culminating in an impressive display of formation headbanging during Ray's solo.

The following month saw the band make a return visit to Britain, where their brief run of shows a year previously had excited the UK music press to the extent that *NME's* Rick Martin declared, 'My Chemical Romance's star quality leaves the rest of the chasing pack choking on their dust.' This time around, a slightly longer tour visited larger venues and received an even more fervent response from British reviewers. In his account of MCR's 4 February show at London's Islington Academy, *Kerrang!*'s Luke Lewis displayed astonishment at the zeal with which the band were greeted by the packed crowd. 'Never before have we seen a room explode with such rabid, obliterating force as My Chemical Romance spark in London tonight. By the end of opener "I'm Not Okay" all sense of decorum and rhythm has already been lost. From front to back it's one huge mosh-pit – a seething, suffocating, red-black sweatstorm that lifts you off your feet and pins you to the wall.'

Three days later, My Chem were on the other side of the planet playing their first headlining gigs in Japan, where they visited Osaka and Nagoya, before wrapping up with a pair of shows in Tokyo. 'You learn a lot from being in Japan,' wrote Gerard in his tour diary for *Punk Rock Confidential* magazine. 'There is a level of respect that you don't find anywhere else in the world and it actually makes you a better person.'

**'Sometimes you have to kind of die inside in order to rise from your own ashes and believe in yourself and love yourself and become a new person.' – Gerard Way**

After a brief stopover in Hawaii, the quintet returned to the US to begin the A Taste of Chaos Tour. Setting out from Orlando, Florida on 18 February, the tour packed 37 dates into six weeks, crossing into Canada and zig-zagging cross-country before terminating in Phoenix, Arizona on 2 April. 'When I saw the route I was scared,' admitted Gerard. Some of those places hold 10,000 or 12,000. I couldn't believe our band had anything to do with pulling that many people.' In addition to support from metalcore combo Killswitch Engage and New Jersey's Senses Fail, MCR were delighted to be touring alongside old road buddies the Used. 'It's awesome touring with the Used,' Gerard told *Kerrang!* 'We've been out with these kids so many times, but it's really exciting now for both our bands.'

As well as continuing their friendship backstage, Gerard and Used frontman Bert McCracken teamed up at the end of each night's show to perform a cover version of the 1981 Queen/David Bowie hit 'Under Pressure'. 'Everybody comes out, everybody plays, it's fucking incredible,' enthused McCracken. 'It's nice singing with Gerard

*Gerard Way – single-handedly responsible for bringing theatricality back to the rock milieu.*

onstage, too. Man, that guy makes me feel good. We want to do a video for "Under Pressure" where it's me and Gerard in bed together.'

The two bands subsequently recorded their version of the song to raise funds for those affected by the tsunami that occurred on 26 December 2004, off the cost of Sumatra, Indonesia. (An undersea earthquake – the second largest ever recorded – had resulted in a series of tidal waves that killed over 180,000 and left nearly 50,000 people unaccounted for.)

Such were the two bands' hectic tour schedules that their individual parts were pasted together, having been recorded separately in London and Los Angeles. 'We had a very small window of opportunity in which to do it,' explained Gerard. 'Two of my guys flew out a day early to L.A. before we started some tour and I was out there and did my vocals. The Used based off of our template of the song, put their parts over it and then it was together.'

> ## 'We know that the video for "Helena" is our chance to be known as a "video" band.' – Gerard Way

Initially released exclusively as a download, with all proceeds going to the disaster relief fund, the song later appeared as a bonus track on the 2005 re-release of the Used's 2004 album, *In Love And Death*. Although downloaded music was ineligible for the official singles chart, the track reached Number 41 on the *Billboard* Hot 100, which draws its listings from airplay as well as conventional sales.

My Chem had also recently achieved a more traditional form of chart success with the single release of 'Helena', which cracked the US Top 40 and British Top 20 in early March. The single was supported by another Marc Webb video, which set the song within the context of a funeral service featuring the band and dancing mourners. The role of the deceased Helena was taken by actress, dancer and burlesque performer Tracy Phillips, who has also appeared in videos for No Doubt, the Offspring and the Goo Goo Dolls. 'The video is very sombre and very depressing – it's about a girl in her twenties who died young, about a tragic young death,' Gerard told MTV's James Montgomery. 'It was emotional making it, so it was nice that so many of our fans could be a part of it too. Pretty much all the mourners at the funeral were our fans. We put out a call on the website, like, "Be in our video," and we got a ton of responses.'

Perhaps the most poignant moment of the promo comes right at the very end: after car-

*A final journey – the symbolic funeral procession for 'Helena', ahead of the band's Astoria concert on 9 April 2005.*

rying the coffin down the church steps the band slide the casket into the back of the waiting hearse. With tragic finality, Gerard closes the door and looks in through the vehicle's small rear window, with just the sound of the rain beating on the car's roof for accompaniment.

Neither over-sentimental nor mawkish, the clip went on to be nominated for five MTV Video Music Awards – a testament to Webb's skill as a filmmaker and the clarity of Gerard's conceptual vision. 'It had to be handled delicately and beautifully,' explained the frontman. 'There's this fine line where I use my pain and suffering to make art, but where does it reach the point where you're exploiting your pain, you know? We got some ridiculous treatments from directors, some to the point of being disrespectful and offensive. Like, I would read them and be like, "Does this person know that this song is about my dead grandmother?"'

After a swift return to the UK for a four-date tour supported by Californian indie band Open Hand, My Chem were invited to support Green Day on the North American Leg of their huge American Idiot tour. 'This is a dream come true. I have wanted to tour with Green Day since I was fifteen,' Frank told the *Iowa State Daily*. 'For them to choose us is mind blowing. [Green Day] is one of those bands that trail-blazed so much. If it weren't for Green Day, bands like us or any band wouldn't be able to reach the heights that we have reached here.'

'The band couldn't believe it when we heard the news,' Gerard recalled. 'I got the call and I was in the street in New York City and it was pouring rain, but I was just yelling and people were staring at me. And that was everybody's response. I think Bob fell down a flight of stairs when he heard the news.'

For Gerard in particular, the invitation to support Green Day was a concrete vali-dation of MCR's worth from one of his all-time musical heroes. 'It's amazing. I think it's safe to say that it's the biggest thing to ever happen to this band,' declared Gerard in an interview for MTV. 'I always cite my influences as being the Misfits and the Smiths and the Cure; those artists inspired me to write music. But Billie Joe from Green Day influenced me to play guitar.'

> 'Lots of people grab my ass. I'm actually starting to get this thing now where people grab my package.' – Gerard Way

'We like a lot of those [newer] bands, and it's flattering to hear you've influenced them,' observed Green Day bassist Mike Dirnt. 'And all of them are going to forge their own path and catalogue and career history someday. But the compliments are kind of hard to take. It's like, "Congratulations, you're old!"'

It's often said that working with one's heroes is something to be approached with great caution; there is unlimited potential for youthful admiration to be shattered by the all-too-human reality. However, Green Day are something of a rarity among globally recog-nised rock icons, remaining reassuringly unaffected by their massive and enduring success. 'They are the nicest guys we've ever met,' asserted Gerard. 'We've never seen a band reach out to us so much in so many ways, in a live set, on a personal level. They really make us feel like fellow musicians. We've toured with bands that were only slightly bigger than us or at our level that acted more like rock stars. They don't even act like rock stars, they're just a punk band and they put on the greatest, greatest fucking show in the world.'

*Drum and bass – Mikey and Bob's rhythmic synergy underpins My Chem's extravagant musical diversity.*

On top of making My Chem welcome on the tour, Green Day frontman Billie Joe Armstrong also took Gerard under his wing, giving the vocalist the benefit of the experience he'd accumulated over the previous decade and a half. 'I had conversations with Gerard,' Armstrong told *Kerrang!* 'He was feeling a bit uncertain at the time and I just told him not to be afraid. I think he was shying away. He was at that point where a band reads too much of its own press, and they start to internalise everything. To the point where they become boring. So I told him that it's okay to be a rock star. It's okay to be that, because the world needs good rock stars. We've got enough boring people.'

'He said the biggest mistake they had made was to be angry about the success,' Gerard explained to *Blender*. 'What I got from him was personal: "Don't hold back; be what you are and don't be ashamed of it. Don't be afraid to take it by the balls."'

My Chem's stint supporting Green Day ran from 15 April through to 20 May 2005, after which they travelled to Malibu, California to shoot a video for 'The Ghost Of You' with director Marc Webb. With a filming budget of

> 'I'm not gonna tell you what to do with your life.' – Gerard Way

$500,000, the three-and-a-half minute promo was the band's most expensive and ambitious yet, and cast My Chem as Second World War G.I.'s. 'The night before the shooting, I slept an hour, because it finally hit me,' Gerard revealed to *Kerrang!*'s Daniel Lukes. 'The band always trusts me. I sat them down and I said, "This is what I think the video should be and it's not going to be cheap" – and they were just like, "Well, what the fuck. We didn't get into it for the money, so let's make a great video."'

Cutting between shots of My Chem performing at a United Services Organisations dance (which saw Gerard fashion his hair into a period quiff, while Ray's afro was slicked down) and footage of a D-Day-style beach landing, the video reaches a moving climax as Mikey is gunned down on the beach and dies, despite Ray's efforts to save him. Fading out amid volleys of artillery and infantry fire, the clip successfully transplants Gerard's lyrical introspection into World War II, with the 'never coming home' refrain serving to accentuate the video's emphasis on the futility of war.

Referencing such films as *Saving Private Ryan* and *Memphis Belle*, the clip continued My Chemical Romance's tradition of making promos that indicated their love of cinema. 'When we talked about making "Ghost of You", we spoke of it being very cin-

*2005 saw Gerard's rock dreams come true as*
*MCR supported his long-time heroes Green Day.*

ematic,' Marc Webb explained. 'Our goal for this was to make it feel like you're watching a film and creating a world. The guitar playing and singing is an organic part of them playing in the USO [United Service Organisations] scene. And there are hand-held battlefield scenes. And there's a huge, epic quality to the piece.'

Shortly after filming had been completed, a rough cut of the video began circulating on the web. Although delighted by the enthusiasm of fans keen to catch a glimpse of the footage, Gerard reacted to the leak with some ambivalence. 'It's not such a bad problem to have people wanting to see our video so badly that they're trying to find it on the internet or leak it. Sure you're bummed artistically, because it's not finished, but it's a pretty awesome problem. There's so much buzz about it that people can't wait.'

However, Frank was less upbeat. 'It's like painting a picture, and you're not done with it yet, but someone shows it in an art exhibit,' the guitarist told MTV. 'It's the art that you make, and if you don't feel that it's done, for people to go and put it on the Internet and have people download it is a bit of a bummer.'

> 'We wanted to create an environment where there wasn't racism or sexism or homophobia.' – Gerard Way

The fourth and final single to be lifted from *Revenge*, 'The Ghost Of You' was subsequently released on 29 August, hitting the Top 30 in the UK and becoming the band's first Top Ten hit in China, where it reached Number 2.

After an all-too-short break, the band flew out to play a short run of European festivals before returning to the US to hook up with the 2005 Warped Tour on 18 June. This year's line-up included ageing former Generation X frontman Billy Idol, pop/punk mainstays the Offspring, ska-punk supergroup the Transplants, and exciting newcomers such as energetic gypsy punks Gogol Bordello.

Older and wiser after the excesses of the previous year, Gerard opted to steer clear of much of the before, during and after-show partying, to sidestep any potential temptations that could knock him off the wagon. 'That first year was fucking hard,' recalled the frontman. 'I'm sure I made a lot of enemies on Warped Tour because I couldn't leave the bus. I'm sure that everyone thought I was being the rock star. But I knew that if one more person waved a bottle of alcohol in front of me I would have gone crazy.'

Whereas in 2004, MCR were the new boys at Warped, this time – thanks to the success of *Three Cheers For Sweet Revenge* and almost a full year of relentless touring – the band were one of the main draws and closed the show on a number of occasions. 'Every

*Uncomfortable on the red carpet, the quintet submit to the glare of publicity at the MTV Video Awards, August 2005.*

time they play, there's more and more kids singing along, and they meet more and more kids that say, "Your band's helped me through some of the hardest, darkest times of my life,"' manager Brian Schechter told *Pollstar*. 'That's why they started the band – to help kids the way that music helped them when they were having tough times.'

Besides getting the group's anti-suicide/self-harm message across, Gerard made a stand against groups who sought to alienate sections of the crowd through sexism, racism and homophobia, or tried to coerce female fans to get their tits out 'for the boys'. 'We encouraged people to throw loose change at anyone alienating people and, in turn, tried to get ignorant bands to stop calling kids "faggots" and call us that instead,' wrote Gerard in his *Spin* Warped Tour diary.

After the tour reached the end of its road in mid-August, My Chem departed for Europe to play a clutch of summer festivals, including a main stage debut at the twin Reading and Leeds events at the end of the month. The band had been scheduled to appear on the second stage at the two bank holiday weekend shows, but were bumped up to the main stage by the organisers, where they appeared on a bill that included Iron Maiden, Marilyn Manson and the Stooges. Delighted with the way in which the buzz around MCR was developing in Britain, Gerard identified the appeal of the band for UK audiences. 'British people really get black humour, and that's one of the strongest elements. I think they heard emo and wanted something different. We are kind of the "What else you got?" of emo.'

> ### 'We don't really have any crazy tour stories.' – Gerard Way

After returning from Europe, My Chem headed across the USA on their biggest headline tour to date. Supported by Alkaline Trio and former New Found Glory touring keyboard player James Dewees' solo project, Reggie and the Full Effect, the five-week run of large venue and arena shows kicked off in Columbus, Ohio on 15 September and wound up in Baltimore, Maryland on 21 October.

In keeping with MCR's desire to 'put on a show', the tour featured an enhanced light show and some big-screen video content. 'We'd talked about bringing out dancers for our headlining tour in the fall, but it's a big undertaking; you have to have a bus full of dancers,' observed Gerard. 'We've always wanted to do a big theatrical tour. But you have to do it in steps. You can't just spring it on people all at once.'

Visually, MCR's adoption of successive band uniforms had underlined the group's collective harmony. 'We're all brothers,' declared Frank in an interview with *Iowa State Daily*'s Darin Longman. 'It's more of a gang. It's the five of us versus the world, so we have a very strong bond.' The band's summer/fall 2005 look included a black bulletproof vest. 'It symbolises the fact that this band feels indestructible,' Gerard explained to *Rock Sound*. 'It's also about us relating to hip-hop artists. We come from the same world as a lot of them, and we relate to their drive and the way they don't give a fuck about what anyone else thinks.'

My Chem rounded out October with an appearance at the annual New Orleans Voodoo Music Festival, which featured a host of contemporary heavyweights such as the Foo Fighters, Nine Inch Nails and Queens of the Stone Age, alongside legendary glam/punk pioneers the New York Dolls, and newer bands like disco-rock hybrids the Bravery.

*Another night, another town – 2005 saw Frank and the band undertake their most intensive gigging schedule thus far.*

The day after the festival, MCR departed for an eight-date headlining tour of the UK's largest concert halls. The gigs were notable for an extraordinary outpouring of affection and support for the band that was as unexpected as it was rapturous. The two sold-out concerts at London's Brixton Academy provided affirmation of just how much momentum their British bandwagon had picked up since they last played the same south London venue, in support of Taking Back Sunday, eleven months earlier. 'Both of the London shows were, honestly, two of the best shows we've played in our entire lives,' enthused Ray. 'The fans were amazing, so genuine about their love of the music – they don't care about looking cool – they just want to have a good time.'

> **'We've mutilated, killed and disembowelled rock'n'roll clichés.' – Frank Iero**

In her enthusiastic five-K review of the show, *Kerrang!*'s Emma Johnston had little doubt that MCR were now in the big league. 'Believe the hype, they *are* that good, so good that this congregation looks set to grow and grow.' 'In the UK, it's like "We're behind you." It's a different vibe at UK shows,' observed Gerard. 'And when we get a great crowd it leads to the best shows. That's how it's been recently. You can't get that on TV or from a video.'

After a brief visit to Dublin, where fans queued from 6am to catch a glimpse of the band, the road-weary quintet returned to the US for a few short, recuperative days, before heading north for a string of eight shows in Canada. Finally, the band re-crossed the border to wrap up their 2005 touring with a show at the Premier in Seattle.

Although audiences across the globe were warming to My Chemical Romance, in late November Bert McCracken went against the flow of popular opinion and declared that his relationship with his former touring buddies was at an end. 'I'd prefer not to say anything about My Chemical Romance, except that we did have a falling out,' the Used frontman told MTV. 'We don't speak at all anymore. It's got nothing to do with their success. I'm completely comfortable with where our band is at. We used to be very close, but no more. We had a falling out. The rest of my band, they're still mates with all the guys in that band.'

Gerard subsequently denied that there was any rift between him and McCracken, telling Australia's *Blunt* magazine, 'That's clearly a press situation, to draw attention. There's nothing wrong with me and him. As far as real beefs, there was never anything real about it.'

However, despite Gerard's efforts to downplay the breakdown in his and Bert's friendship, McCracken seemed determined to widen the rift, refuting claims that the dispute was media-generated and explaining the genesis of his antipathy toward MCR to *Blunt*. 'It was maybe like a year and a half ago I saw all their heads blow up and after their heads blew up their heads kinda went up their arses as well. And I just thought, "Fuck that, I don't need friends like that and I don't even need acquaintances like that." As far [as] the whole thing goes now, I wish them the best with their touring and their record, but it's over. It's definitely not a publicity stunt.'

Speaking to *Blender* the following year, Gerard revealed that McCracken had turned on the band during the San Diego leg of the 2005 Warped Tour. 'It was really unfortunate. We were about to take the stage and he was standing with a megaphone trying to get kids not to watch us. We just hit the feedback and drowned him out.'

Whereas Gerard has subsequently made little reference to the feud, several songs on the Used's 2007 album, *Lies For The Liars*, have been identified as referring to the dispute, with the song 'Pretty Handsome Awkward' believed by many to be specifically directed at the My Chem vocalist.

Despite this minor ruckus, 2005 had been a massive success for MCR, with their constant touring inspiring new fans to pick up the group's back catalogue and sending their popularity skyrocketing to levels that the quintet could scarcely have imagined possible fifteen months earlier. 'I think, what drew us in the beginning was the fact that we get to see the entire world. We had always hoped to see just the country and then we got the opportunity to see the whole world, and we have really,' Gerard reflected. 'I think that's what drew us, the fact that we weren't gonna just be these guys that lived in our parents' basements anymore, we're gonna be guys who saw the world and experienced things and grew up a lot as people.'

'It is really nice to be accepted and loved,' he explained to the *MusicPix* website's Gwyn Tyme. 'So we just take it as it comes so we're able to stay very humble about it. It was also something that we were never concerned with. We were all loners and outcasts in some ways and we still feel like that.'

# Chapter 9

# US VS. THEM

'Nobody's in the middle with us. It's either "I love them" or "I want to kill them." People love us and believe in us, or they want to see us destroyed. And I love that.'
– Gerard Way

Although it was destined to become the biggest, and in some respects the most difficult, year in My Chemical Romance's career to date, 2006 began quietly. During their extended touring sojourn, the quintet had worked on new material whenever the opportunity arose. 'We had a makeshift studio in the back of our bus,' explained Frank. 'A lot of the stuff we wrote on the road we kind of scrapped. Maybe one or two songs we kept or just kept in the back of our heads to write later. Most of them were just to get the writing process going.' Such creative filtering enabled the group to develop, taking their established sound into new areas. 'The benefit of writing so much on the road when every other band was partying was that we got *Revenge* part two out of our systems,' Gerard told *Blender*.

With the quintet's touring commitments fulfilled, My Chem took a well-deserved break before reconvening in New York to initiate pre-production work for their third album. 'We always have our own pre and this is when we make decisions about what we want to bring to the producer,' recounted Gerard in an interview with Dublin-based radio station Phantom FM's Peter Vamos.

It was during these brainstorming sessions that the concepts that would comprise

*The Black Parade: My Chemical Romance's macabre, theatrical alter ego.*

the basis of *The Black Parade* began to coalesce. 'The intention was to make something that was classic, something timeless,' Ray told *Alternative Press* journalist Scott Heisel. 'Something that, 20 or 30 years from now, parents could play for their kids and say, "This is what I was listening to when I was your age. Check it out – it's still fucking cool." We wanted to make a record you could pass down. There's a lot of music out now that doesn't feel like that.'

Such lofty conceptualising led Gerard to revisit his original, unrealised aspirations for *Revenge*. 'I always wanted to make a very theatrical, almost Broadway record, with grand themes and epic sounds, extra sound effects, marching bands, bells and whistles. I knew I wanted to do that but I knew it wasn't the right time, I knew we hadn't grown enough as a band, and we hadn't gotten Bob as a drummer yet.'

> **'I just want to kind of give the world something special.' – Gerard Way**

In order to realise Gerard's grand design for the disc, it was vital that the group hire a producer in tune with the frontman's vision. 'We needed a guy who'd actually captured show tunes,' recalled Gerard. The ideal candidate was Rob Cavallo, who, in addition to producing five Green Day albums (including *American Idiot* and *Dookie*) and working with diverse acts ranging from Fleetwood Mac to L7, had also produced the soundtrack to the hit musical *Rent*. 'Going into this record we met Rob Cavallo and when talking with him, he was so passionate about music, about music in general, not just certain songs,' recalled Frank.

With Cavallo immediately grasping what Gerard was striving for in terms of the album's diversity and grandeur, there was little question of any other producers being considered. 'The only band he wanted to produce this year was us. We knew the record we were going to make and we knew he was the guy that was going to capture that,' the vocalist told *Disorder* magazine. The producer immediately set about exploring the album's conceptual landscape with his new charges. 'One of the more immediate goals that we discussed with Rob Cavallo was to create this world in your head,' recalled Gerard in an interview with Jim DeRogatis of the *Chicago Sun-Times*. 'The biggest goal was to not make a record that was self-absorbed, but to make a record that was self-aware . . . to really create the loudest, ultimate form of self-expression that hasn't been heard in a long time.'

With My Chem's ambitions for the new album matching the stratospheric levels of expectation among their hardcore following, there was a danger that they could have been placing themselves under a burdensome amount of pressure as they began laying down tracks with Cavallo in mid-April. 'The only pressure that we have ever put on ourselves for this whole process was to write the best record we could,' observed Ray. 'People will have their own opinions and expectations, but you can't feel that. The furthest thing from our minds is how the record does [in terms of sales].'

Rather than feeling apprehensive, Bob Bryar was relishing his first opportunity to record as a member of MCR. 'It's just something that we had all dreamed of for our whole lives, having the opportunity to make a record like this and finding the people that can make it happen for us,' the drummer told the *New Zealand Herald* in December 2006.

Instead of booking time at a regular studio complex, My Chem opted to isolate themselves from any possible distractions by checking into the Canfield-Moreno estate near Micheltorena, Los Angeles. Also known as the Paramour Mansion, the huge Mediterranean-style building was constructed in 1923 by the architect Robert Farquhar for silent movie heartthrob Antonio Moreno, who had recently married oil heiress Daisy Canfield-Danziger.

The couple's marriage lasted just ten years. A week after they formally separated due to 'temperamental differences', in February 1933, Daisy was killed when her car plunged some 250 feet down a cliff. It subsequently emerged that the driver, a young Swiss national named Dussac, had become disorientated by a particularly heavy bank of fog. Despite suffering multiple vertebrae fractures, Dussac survived to drag himself back to the road and flag down a passing vehicle. Once the incident was made public, unsubstantiated rumours began to circulate to the effect that Daisy was murdered, with the accident somehow contrived by her recently estranged husband.

> '**I would love to be able to turn invisible.' – Mikey Way**

Subsequently, the Canfield-Moreno Estate became the venue for a series of alleged sightings of a ghost believed to be the earthbound spirit of Daisy, who had been buried on the property. The advent of talking motion pictures had led to a decline in Moreno's career, as his heavy Spanish accent made him unsuitable for many roles. As his finances waned, Moreno sold the mansion for $200,000 to a foundation who used the complex to establish a school for underprivileged girls. Later it was converted into a convent for Franciscan nuns.

After the estate was damaged by an earthquake measuring 6.0 on the Richter scale in October 1987, the order sold the property and it fell into a state of some disrepair. In 1998 the complex was acquired by philanthropist and developer Dana Hollister, who renamed it the 'Paramour' and set about transforming it into an upmarket residence, film location and recording studio. In addition to being used by filmmakers such as David Lynch and the Coen brothers, the Paramour's grounds have hosted concerts by artists such as Elton John, Beck and the Red Hot Chili Peppers.

Among those who used the estate's recording facilities were nu-metal survivors Papa Roach, who resided there from October 2005 to June 2006 during the recording of their fourth studio album, *The Paramour Sessions*. 'The whole property was completely fucking haunted, and I saw it as a sanctioned opportunity for me to lose my mind,' claimed Roach drummer Dave Bruckner. 'I was visited by inter-dimensional beings, had out-of-body sex with spirits from old Hollywood, learned how to see spectres, and now know what it feels like to have a ghost walk through me. It's a very enlightening and inspiring experience, and something to check off the list.'

'The place is definitely haunted,' Gerard told *Revolver*. 'Doors would slam, and the faucets would turn on. You'd get a bath drawn for you of freezing cold water in your room, and you wouldn't know why.' The Paramour was also unnaturally cold. 'It was very strange, since it was very hot outside but only 40°F inside,' recalled Bob. 'We wore jackets all day long and bought every space heater in the Los Angeles area.'

> **'I don't want people to be afraid of living, which I think is everybody's biggest fear.' – Gerard Way**

Whereas Gerard was mildly fascinated by the estate's eerie ambience and channelled some of these vibes into his songwriting, Mikey found the environment wholly oppressive. 'I was especially scared of my room. I don't know what colour the walls were because there was never any light in there, but it had this one blue light bulb which just made the room glow,' he told *Rock Sound*. 'Every day you'd wake up and get scared because you wouldn't know where you were. I was so scared that I would sneak into Gerard's room and sleep on the floor.'

During the two months that the band were ensconced within the Paramour, Gerard developed his vision of a theatrically expressive album with a sequential narrative featuring a central character – the Patient – who reflects upon his life as he prepares to die from cancer. 'I started to envision the Patient as a character being in his thirties,' Gerard revealed in an interview for New Zealand's *Real Groove* magazine. 'What would I be feeling if I had done nothing with myself at that point and come down with a terrible

*Mikey and Gerard bring the intensity of* The Black Parade *to the UK, February 2007.*

disease? What if it all got taken away from me? I think a lot of it was the sense of really accomplishing something in my life, to a point where I've seen a lot of stuff and if I died tomorrow, I could be really happy – it was looking at the opposite of that.'

During his dying moments, the Patient drifts into a reverie wherein he remembers his happiest time – being taken to a parade by his father as a young boy. Like many of Gerard's lyrics, this element was drawn from the vocalist's own personal experience. 'I have a really strong memory of my dad taking me and Mikey to a parade,' he explained to *Rolling Stone*'s Austin Scaggs. 'I remember the big inflatable balloons – even the ones of cartoon characters I loved – were so imposing. So I wouldn't say that was my happiest memory, but there's something really cultural about a parade, which is why it became the perfect vehicle. It could represent a funeral procession, or the Day of the Dead or a celebration. For the album's character, it's what he wants death to be.'

With Gerard's creative focus fixated upon death and dying, he too became subject to the Paramour's uniquely unsettling atmosphere. 'I suffered from anxiety and I was only getting three hours sleep a night. One night I woke up and felt like I was being strangled,' he revealed in an interview with *The Sun*'s Jaqui Swift. 'It was something that inhabited the place. I had been writing notes every night and that night I wrote, "We are all just a Black Parade." I thought it would make a great album title.'

**'I think of *The Black Parade* as putting yourself in a straitjacket and jumping into a river, and I like that.' – Gerard Way**

Although the *Black Parade* concept was taking shape, the development of individual album tracks became a difficult process, undermined by the cloying sense of desperation engendered by My Chem's surroundings. 'Sometimes it almost felt like we were haunting the house,' Gerard observed. 'Other people go there because it's cool and haunted and they can have parties. We don't party, so it was just us. It was a very isolated, scary feeling to be like ghosts in this place with no purpose, aimlessly wandering around. Some people wouldn't even come out of their rooms. But at a certain point it felt like it was the only thing there for us, the only company we had.'

In order to break free of the gathering *ennui*, the quintet embarked upon extended sessions of discursive soul-searching. 'We talked about everything – life, us, everything,' Gerard told *Kerrang!* 'Every day we were finding something new and ugly about ourselves. We kept finding things about our personalities that we didn't like. We found all the cracks, all the chinks in our armour. We really found out how ugly we were. But, without that, we couldn't have made a good record. We had to push ourselves right to the edge.'

In addition to the psychologically exacting group therapy sessions, the quintet continued to place themselves under extreme pressure to produce an album of the highest possible quality. 'If it wasn't like staring into the sun with your eyelids cut off, it wasn't good enough for the record,' asserted Gerard.

In any circumstances, being in a closed environment under considerable professional and mental duress would present a huge challenge to most people. For Mikey, who was struggling more than anyone else to come to terms with the isolated nature of the Paramour complex, it all proved too much. 'It was too much stimulus at once. I never had a chance to come to grips with anything – my grandmother dying, my father having a [non-fatal]

heart attack on our tour bus. I was a complete mess,' he recalled. 'Take a manic-depressive kid and throw him in a haunted house – with no cell-phone service, no TV, no heat – and put him in a room with one glowing blue light. I got there immediately and was like, "I know I'm not going to make it through this, I just wonder how it's going to end."'

Thanks in part to a heady cocktail of booze and antidepressants, the bassist began to disengage from the recording process, drifting off into a private world during sessions and prone to uncontrollable crying fits. It was evident that, for the sake of his own well-being, Mikey would have to remove himself from the oppressive pressure-cooker atmosphere that had developed within the Paramour. 'It was like, I'm either gonna leave the band, or I'm gonna leave the planet Earth, or I'm gonna disappear and nobody's gonna hear from me again,' he revealed to *Entertainment Today*'s Whitney Pastorek.

Before Mikey reached complete meltdown, MCR lawyer and unofficial den-mother Stacy Fass intervened, putting the troubled bassist up at her home and arranging for him to see a number of psychologists in order to diagnose and address the root of his depression – which

> 'It takes me a while to tell stories – I think it's because I was drunk for three years.' – Gerard Way

turned out to be a bipolar disorder. 'Getting out of Paramour was the turning point for me. The house had just escalated everything in my head and made everything a million times worse,' Mikey told *Kerrang!* 'My friend Stacy saved my life. She got me out of the house, she put me up at her place and kicked me out of bed and made me go to my therapy appointments. She made me get active help . . . I was seeing four different doctors a week. They were two steps away from putting me into a hospital.'

While Mikey was recovering, the rest of the band struggled to carry on with the album. 'I became extremely edgy and angry,' admitted Gerard. 'We had something we wanted to bring to the world and we were basically forced to stop creating it. It was as if a plug had been pulled. It was a really dark period.'

Once again, Gerard found that songwriting provided the perfect cathartic outlet for the mixture of anger, frustration and anxiety he was experiencing. The immediate result of this was 'Famous Last Words'. 'When it was first written, I know Gerard was very, very angry and desperate,' revealed Ray. 'Mikey had been out of the house for a while and hadn't been writing, and it was a tough time. And the first lyrics he came up with – "But where's your heart / But where's your heart?" – were his expression of the anger and confusion he was feeling about the whole situation.' Mikey subsequently returned to the studio as a non-resident, and the anguished tone of the song took on a more positive aspect. 'When I came back it became triumphant,' he explained. 'And "Famous Last Words" is the anthem.'

> **'I came in and told them, "Let's push it as far as we can go."
> That really opened their eyes. Once they had that kind of freedom
> they loved it.' – Rob Cavallo**

With Mikey coming to terms with his depression and the band back to full strength, My Chem began firing on all cylinders. Tracks such as 'Cancer' and 'Welcome To The Black Parade' were recorded with vigour and purpose. As well as Mikey's return, Rob Cavallo's experience and enthusiasm played a huge part in guiding the band out of their creative difficulties. 'He was *so* hands on with everything and so hands on with every member that he became the part of the band that we've been missing,' enthused Frank. 'He really supported us in everything we wanted to do. He wanted us to take risks, take our time, and to really explore . . . He became part of the family. That was an amazing process.'

For his part, Cavallo believed that the end result justified all the tribulations that MCR faced down during the *Black Parade* sessions. 'You always have to pay a price if you're going to go really deep into the creativity of a band,' observed the producer. 'It makes a band stronger.'

With the creation of *The Black Parade* monopolising the band's energy throughout the first half of 2006, the expanding ranks of MCR fans had to make do with enjoying their heroes via other media.

*Gerard salutes the crowd – as MCR have developed, so their gigs have become rapturous celebrations of the two-way relationship between band and audience.*

March 2006 saw the release of *Life On The Murder Scene*, an audio-visual smorgasbord of all things My Chem, comprising a CD mixing live cuts with unreleased demos and two DVDs – one of which was a candid and revealing road diary. 'It's a documentary that captures the rise and occasional stumblings of this band,' explained Gerard. 'It's really crazy, we had forgotten about a lot of the stuff that happens in the film, like backstage stuff and concert footage. Basically, it tells the story of one really crazy year in this band's life.' The second DVD drew together live footage, TV appearances and the 'I'm Not Okay', 'Helena' and 'Ghost Of You' videos, complete with 'Making Of' featurettes.

The mostly live CD was met with praise from *Rolling Stone*'s Jenny Eliscu, who awarded the compilation a moderate three stars but praised the band's energy. '*Life On The Murder Scene* pulls all the right guns from My Chem's arsenal of songs. As live albums go, this one is A-O-fucking-K.'

> **'I really just didn't want to go back into the hospital. I got caught trying to sneak out of the emergency room.' – Bob Bryar**

As well as the more traditional fare of CDs and DVDs, MCR fans could pick up a novel piece of merchandise thanks to licensed toy specialists SEG Toys, who issued a series of My Chemical Romance action figures both as a set and individually. Depicting the band as five-inch plastic icons, the figures immortalised Gerard, Mikey, Ray, Frank and Bob in realistically posable vinyl. 'I don't think that having a My Chemical Romance action figure will make a kid start his own band,' quipped Gerard. 'I like to think it will make him save children from a burning building.'

With *The Black Parade* set for release in late October, and speculation concerning its closely guarded nature at fever pitch, My Chem began August with a video shoot for 'Welcome To The Black Parade' and 'Famous Last Words', two numbers earmarked as the first singles from the album.

Although My Chem surprisingly chose to break from their successful association with Marc Webb, the hiring of director Samuel Bayer demonstrated the scope of the band's visual ambitions. Responsible for Nirvana's epoch-making 'Smells Like Teen Spirit', the New York-born filmmaker had also worked with rock legends Ozzy Osbourne, Aerosmith and the Ramones. With a dual career as a successful director of major corporate TV adverts, Bayer was well established as one of the medium's most in-demand personnel. Furthermore, he had worked extensively with Green Day, spearheading seven of their videos and directing the Californian trio's concert DVD, *Bullet In A Bible.*

Bayer's treatment for the 'Welcome To The Black Parade' promo brought to life Gerard's album concept, with former child actor Lucas Haas (best known for his role in the 1985 thriller *Witness*, which starred Harrison Ford) cast in the role of *The Black Parade*'s central character, the Patient. 'The whole thing was really fun,' Haas enthused. 'I was wandering around on the stage, and I got to wear all this face paint. It was kind of like Halloween. But the best part was hanging out with the guys in the band and getting to listen to their record over and over again. It was really great. It sort of reminds me of some of the best aspects of theatrical rock and glam.'

Filmed in the same early twentieth-century French impressionist cinema style employed by Jonathan Dayton and Valerie Faris for their evocative visualisation of the Smashing Pumpkins' 'Tonight, Tonight', Bayer's film introduces the quintet in their collective alter ego of the Black Parade. This new group persona, redolent of Bowie's Ziggy Stardust and the Spiders from Mars, saw My Chem take on a radical new look – composed of black drummer boy outfits, with Gerard sporting a short peroxide hairstyle, and Mikey fresh from laser optical surgery which eliminated his need to wear spectacles. Asked about Gerard's new look by *Rip It Up* magazine's Scott McLennan, Bob explained that the frontman viewed the role of the Patient as an exercise in method acting. 'He got so into singing and being in this mindset of his character called the Patient that he cut off all his hair and dyed it. Even some of the stuff he sings, you can tell where his head was at the time.'

When asked by *FasterLouder.com* about the rationale behind the creation of these new identities, Mikey observed, 'It was a really difficult album for us to make and there was a certain point where it was so dark that it felt like we really needed to become much more than brothers – we needed to become a new band.'

Initially issued on 11 September 2006 as a download, 'Welcome To The Black Parade' provided eager fans with their first indications of what was to follow on the album. The anthemic number mixes elements of grandiose prog/glam and Green Day-style pop/punk with Gerard's expressive lyrics, to create a track that is a bombastic *reveille* for the MCRmy. 'It was really a call to arms for our army, for our kids, but not delivering the message of "we're going to fight using violence or we're gonna destroy everything,"' explained Gerard. 'We're not preaching hate or aggression, we're saying let's buck the stereotype. Instead of feeling sorry for ourselves, let's stop crying and show the world how strong we are.'

Originally titled 'The Five Of Us Are Dying', 'Welcome To The Black Parade' is a texturally rich, multi-tracked number that underwent constant revision during the album sessions. For Bob, the painstaking way in which the song was built up, combined with the psychological and emotional travails the quintet underwent during the creative process, meant that its final realisation had far more significance than if it had come together quickly and easily. 'That's just a personal thing,' observed the drum titan. 'Because we went through changing that song a million times in the studio. It was really hard to finish, and when we finally did it was just amazing.'

With Ray Toro once again demonstrating his mastery of the Brian May tab book to spectacular effect, many critics were quick to compare him with the Queen guitar legend. With customary humility, the MCR guitarist took such observations as compliments. 'I appreciate it,' he told *Rocky Mountain News* journalist Mark Brown. 'He's one of my favourite guitarists. I just love his work. I love how he takes guitar and makes it very symphonic. That guy is capable of everything. He can lay back when he needs to, then writes some of the best leads. He comes up with great harmonies, he's a great singer. To me it's an honour for anybody to say that I play like him or the parts remind them of Queen.'

Released on CD three weeks ahead of the album on 2 October 2006, 'Welcome To The Black Parade' topped the *Billboard* Modern Rock charts, the UK singles chart, and made Number 1 in New Zealand, Israel and the Philippines.

The second leg of MCR's two-day session with Samuel Bayer saw My Chem reprise their roles as the Black Parade for a more straightforward performance shoot of 'Famous Last Words'. Cast as weary soldiers amidst a barren, flame-blasted landscape, the film emphasises the emotional intensity of the song.

Although it would subsequently be released in January 2007 as the second single from *The Black Parade*, in the context of the album 'Famous Last Words' represents the final instalment in the saga of the Patient. 'He starts to plead with death and beg for a second chance and thinks that, "If I only had this one more shot, I would be so much different, I would really live life to the utmost,"' explained Frank. 'So you're left with this feeling of hope.'

'At first I thought [the Patient had died], but the more I think about it, the more I think he's not dead,' Gerard told the *New York Times*. 'Maybe this is all in his head. Maybe he can fight. Now I think he has a choice to live.'

At the very end of the video, Bob can be heard saying, 'I can't take this fucking heat any more,' as he remained at his drum kit for as long as possible, while the flames erupt around him. Able to endure the heat no longer, he staggers away from the conflagration and can be seen examining a burn on the back of his left calf. 'I got a third degree burn on my leg that got infected, which then infected my blood and gave me a staph [*staphylococcus aureus* – a bacterial skin contamination] infection,' Bob revealed to *Rip It Up*. 'I had an abscess on the side of my face that put pressure on my brain and it got out of hand. I was admitted to the hospital for a while, but it's all cleared up now though I think. I got a sweet scar out of it though.'

Initially, Bob's injury was considered to be nasty, but not serious, and, despite having to cancel a show in San Diego, the quintet flew to England for a short run of gigs and publicity appearances.

However, by the time the band had returned to the US at the end of the month, Bob's calf 'looked like guacamole'. It was obvious that the burn had become badly infected, and the unfortunate drummer was rushed into hospital. 'I thought I'd be there for ten minutes, but as soon as they saw me, they got all serious and gave me an IV and said they'd have to do a CAT scan. They did all these blood tests and kept me there for fourteen hours,' Bob recalled in an interview for *Revolver*. 'The whole thing was such a nightmare. This doctor stuck my cheek with a needle about six inches long and the width of an IV tube. Then he went in and out of the inside of my mouth with the needle about ten times.'

> **'Our fans are really smart, and they understand where we're coming from.' – Frank Iero**

Had the infection been allowed to spread any further, it could potentially have been life-threatening. As it was, Bob was kept in for monitoring, which necessitated the cancellation of gigs in New York and Pennsylvania. 'We didn't realise just how serious it was at first and Bob even tried to check out of hospital as he wanted to play the shows we were forced to cancel,' recalled Gerard. 'It was a scary moment as we were so engrossed in the notion of death that when Bob nearly died, it was like it was a dream, well, a nightmare. We're all just happy he pulled through.'

'If it's easy, it's not My Chem,' laughed Frank. 'We always find the way to make it the most difficult thing in the world. If there's not a way to get hurt doing it or if it's not overly difficult, I'm sorry, we have to pass. For the next video, I think we're going to release lions and have them [devour] us. We don't like it easy.'

Despite Bob being hampered by his rapidly worsening leg infection, and Gerard nursing an injured ankle picked up at the same shoot, the band's whistle-stop jaunt to England was hardly uneventful. The more compact nature of the UK music scene meant that the rapid increase in My Chemical Romance's popularity was far more evident than in the US, which is not so prone to the hot-housing effect generated by a national media.

As the band were touching down in England, the *Daily Mail* prepared to run an article entitled 'Emo Cult Warning For Parents'. The piece identified My Chemical Romance and Green Day as being the most popular bands among 'the Emos', a cult that *Mail* journalist Sarah Sands described as being 'a cool, young sub-set of the Goths', observing that this cultural phenomenon involved 'a celebration of self harm'.

Not allowing her complete misinterpretation of contemporary popular culture to get in the way of a righteous moral panic, Sands showed a comprehensive lack of insight into My Chem, Green Day, and an emo scene that was not only a thing of the past, but also totally removed from her hysterical description of a youthful death cult.

Published on 16 August 2006, the piece runs through a number of sweeping generalisations, from which anxious parents may determine whether or not their offspring have embarked on a path that can

> 'It doesn't matter who's a saviour for whom. It's almost like, if you believe I am, then I am to you.' – Gerard Way

only end in whey-faced, black-clad doom. In keeping with those who make ill-informed comments because they are apart from popular youth culture rather than a part of it, Sands also makes the most astonishing assertions – 'There is also a deadly glamour about the Goths. The word femme-fatale is Goth based. Many of the alluring women of our time – Nigella Lawson, Debbie Harry, Chrissie Hynde, Sophie Ellis Bextor, Lily Allen – have a touch of the Goth about them.'

Rather than stir up the anticipated shock-horror furore among less mentally agile parents, Sands' article ultimately succeeded in creating a debate about how the British media demonises youth and youth culture. Articles such as those by experienced *Guardian* rock critic Alexis Petridis cited the *Mail* piece as an example of inaccurate and overly-subjective journalism: 'the Daily Mail's article has proved hard to ignore,' he wrote. 'That's partly because it was so shrill and barmy.'

However, despite the all-too-obvious flaws within Sands' article, there were those whose distaste for My Chem allowed them to embrace such strident scaremongering. After a successful opening to their short visit to England – including a showcase gig at the Hammersmith Palais, complete with a Black Parade street procession outside the venue, and the receipt of *Kerrang!*'s 'Best Band On The Planet' award – MCR returned to the Reading festival to be met by a hail of bottles and debris.

Despite having to duck everything from golf balls to that most ubiquitous of Reading missiles – the urine-filled plastic bottle – Gerard remained upbeat and unfazed by the experience. 'That was our greatest victory as a show,' he grinned. 'This band was always about facing adversity. We got bottled for being dangerous. We oppose everything that's conventional about rock'n'roll in this country, our home country, everywhere in the world. That weekend, kids were getting beat up in the audience, the guys on stage were getting beat up, and we got through it, just like the kids got through it.

'The ironic thing about the *Daily Mail* and Reading is that they both involved people who wanted to silence the band but what happened was the direct opposite,' he asserted in an interview with *Kerrang!* 'It actually made us explode in the UK to a much bigger level than before, it gave us such a voice. That's what happens when people try to shut you up, you just get a lot louder.'

Also keen to jump on the anti-My Chem bandwagon were Leicestershire quartet Kasabian, who had seen MCR leapfrog them in the Reading running order the previous year. Like Sarah Sands, Kasabian vocalist Tom Meighan was woefully out of touch with the MCR ethos, observing, 'They don't have anything positive to say. The only good news is that it won't last. These clowns won't be around for much longer. Their make-up will flake off and the scene will die out. And it can't happen soon enough.'

Of course, it's possible that Meighan was simply using My Chemical Romance as a means of securing his band some welcome column inches. 'That just makes them [sound] kinda ignorant,' retorted Gerard. 'This band has never had a bullshit war ever. I haven't found an opponent worthy enough yet. If you're gonna take me on, you'd better have the balls for it! If you're gonna talk shit about us, you'd better have the juice. And we haven't found anybody with the juice yet.'

MCR returned to the US at the end of August, rounding out an action-packed month by opening the MTV Video Music Awards with a performance of 'Welcome To The Black Parade', from the top of the 872-foot General Electric Building, part of New York's Rockefeller complex. 'It was so high up that you were more nervous about that,' recalled Gerard. 'We were so far removed from any stressful situation. We weren't backstage at any awards show, so it was just us and this camera crew and these kids on top of this building.'

As My Chem looked down on the glittering lights of the Big Apple from their lofty perch, it must have seemed they had arrived at the top of the world. The imminent release of *The Black Parade* could prove decisive in confirming or dispelling such a notion.

# Chapter 10

# THE PERPETUAL CABARET

**'I tried to remain a child for so long, and I think I'm over that and want to deal with real shit.'**
**– Gerard Way**

Described by Bob as MCR's 'defining record', *The Black Parade* got its US release on 24 October 2006. Speaking in that month's *Rock Sound*, Frank was bullish about the album: 'I really can't wait for people to hear what we have done. I am so proud of what we have accomplished on this record. Nothing can overshadow it. Nothing. Once you hear it you will understand how much time and effort has gone into making it; when you hear this record you will hear the blood pumping thorough our veins, you will hear the heartbeat of everyone that worked on the record and you will hear Rob as the sixth member of the band.'

Originally entitled 'Father', *Black Parade* opener 'The End' ushers in the album's narrative via the portentous mechanism of a beeping heart monitor. Backed by a lone acoustic guitar, Gerard's opening verse calls to mind the same sense of impending catastrophe as in David Bowie's 'Five Years'. Suddenly, the song expands like an ageing sun, in a burst of noise and flamboyant grandeur reminiscent of Queen, or the Electric Light Orchestra. 'The End' clearly establishes the musical and lyrical parameters of what is to follow, with Gerard cast as a cosmic carnival barker, inducing his audience to join him for the greatest show on earth – the life and death show. 'There's really no

*Gerard brings the saga of 'the Patient' to life in Philadelphia, February 2007.*

turning back for the band after this track,' asserted Gerard. 'It opens up to a big world, but it also paints us into a corner and says, "You've got to stay in this room now."'

'It just had such an epic feel,' recalled Ray in an interview with *Rocky Mountain News*' Mark Brown. 'From the opening line it just sounded like Gerard was getting ready to tell a story. That was when we first talked about doing a concept record. The material we were writing was just getting more and more exciting, a little crazier than the next. Each song progressively got a little weirder, a little more fun.'

'The End' segues with frictionless ease into 'Dead!', as the Patient's heart-monitor flatlines. One of the few songs to survive the cull of material that had been recorded on the road, the song had originally been composed on the previous year's Warped Tour. 'Gerard kept talking about the song "Mr Blue Sky" by ELO. One of the things we wanted to capture was that bouncy pulse that "Mr Blue Sky" has,' recalled Ray.

In context, 'Dead!' documents the moment at which the Patient is told he only has a limited time left to live, and explores his acceptance of the transitory nature of existence. 'To ignore death and to be afraid of it is dumb because everyone is going to face it at some point,' observed Ray in an interview with the Canadian website *Dose*'s Christine Clarke. 'If you look at death and the reality of it, you realise that we're all going to die, so let's use this time on Earth to be positive and do good things. That's the point of this record.'

## 'Some of the topics that we do deal with are very dark topics, but we tend to find the beauty in some of the tragedy.' – Frank Iero

However, the track also has an underlying meaning. 'It's about being dead and people not liking you – it was a commentary on the band and how some people feel about us,' Gerard told *Kerrang!*'s Tom Bryant. 'It's a defiant song. We wanted to say, "You may hate us, but we're still here, more daring and more defiant than ever."'

A plaintive chunk of driving pop/punk, 'This Is How I Disappear' sees the Patient reflecting upon his closest personal relationships. 'There's another character here, a woman who is visiting him in the hospital, even though they're not together anymore,' Gerard explained. 'This song is him telling her, "I've got to go away, without you I'm nearly nothing, yet we still can't be together." It's about regret: "I'm gonna leave now and I know I wasn't the best person."'

Founded upon the bedrock of Mikey's driving bassline, 'The Sharpest Lives' again ties

*Sound and vision – Mikey's laser eye surgery enabled him to dispense with his trademark glasses.*

the album's narrative to My Chem's own back story. A pounding account of drunken revelries and subsequent repentance, the song makes reference to Gerard's battle to overcome his drink problem, while also advancing the Patient's process of remembrance. Speaking to the *NME* in November 2006, clinical psychologist Linda Blair, from the University of Bath, explained that Gerard's device of having the Patient re-examine his life while on his deathbed was grounded in actuality. 'When people have a terminal illness, they gather together all their memories and try to make a story out of it . . . We need to feel that there was a reason we lived. We have to feel that we have worth and there's some sense to our lives. We make an order out of something that didn't necessarily make sense.'

After the bombastic clarion call of 'Welcome To The Black Parade', 'I Don't Love You' sees My Chem demonstrating their mastery of the stadium rock ballad. Destined to become the third single from the album, the lyrical content of the song marks one of the few points on *The Black Parade* where there's no connection between Gerard's words and the Patient's story. Despite this, the sense of loss and regret imparted by Gerard's vocal, and supported by some sensitive keyboard work from experienced synthesizer wizard Jamie Muhoberac, is entirely is entirely in keeping with the album's poignant character. '"I Don't Love You" was very much inspired by Creedence Clearwater's "Who'll Stop The Rain",' revealed Ray, whose bravura soloing again graces the track. 'It's one of our favourite songs, and we tried to capture that vibe – the jangly open chords and stuff.'

> 'All this self-doubt bullshit is a thing of the past, trust me.' – Gerard Way

For a track that affords the Patient some terrifying glimpses of a possible afterlife, it's appropriate that the sonic provenance of 'House Of Wolves' can be found in the mutant voodoo rhythms of rockabilly. 'That was one of the things that came up in pre. Frank had brought the initial riff in and he was very proud of this kind of thing, 'cos he's like, "its something that my dad would have like me to write,"' Gerard told *Disorder* magazine. 'It's based in that traditional almost rockabilly sound, we needed a sound that really felt like Hell and [this] thing does. Rockabilly makes you get a sense of flames.'

In stark contrast to the high-octane devil rock of 'House Of Wolves' comes 'Cancer', which begins with Gerard singing over a simple yet emotionally potent piano melody. Gradually, the song builds as orchestral overdubs combine with vocal harmonies again reminiscent of mid-1970s ELO. This exquisitely complex wall of sound is juxtaposed against the honest brutality of lyrics like, 'Baby, I'm just soggy from the chemo/but counting down the days to go.'

The taboo subject matter ensured that 'Cancer' was always likely to be *The Black Parade's* most controversial number. Gerard was quick to underline the importance of confronting distasteful realities. 'I was tired of talking and bringing a message between the songs, I wanted to bring a message in the songs,' he observed. 'We didn't want to pull punches with this song, but we also didn't want it to seem like it was shock value. I feel the song is very moving and empowering. Within the context of the album, the song also serves to heighten the sense of hopelessness that engulfs the Patient as he prepares to die.'

*Live and direct – Gerard responds to the Marysville CA crowd, July 2007.*

In an album packed so full of changes in style, tempo and pace that there is no such thing as a generic My Chemical Romance song, 'Mama' is yet another clear demonstration of the band's musical diversity. Beginning with the kind of imaginative fusion of European folk, rock and sound effects that underpins Eugene Hutz's Gogol Bordello collective, the track quickly develops into a pastiche of the Bertolt Brecht/Kurt Weill compositions that influenced the 1972 film *Cabaret*. 'There's really a wide range of influences throughout the record,' confirmed Gerard. '"Mama" was inspired by "Alabama Song" by the Doors, which was written by Kurt Weill.' The movie, which was loosely based on a Broadway stage show from six years earlier, starred Liza Minnelli in the role of Sally Bowles, a nightclub singer in Weimar Republic-era Berlin. Fittingly

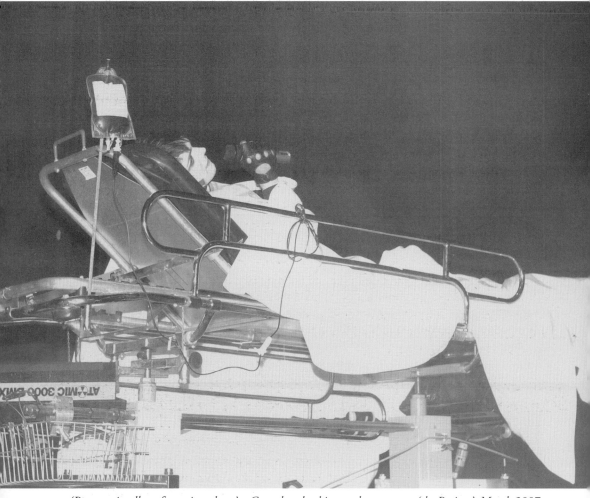

*'Bury me in all my favourite colours' – Gerard makes his grand entrance as 'the Patient', March 2007.*

enough, Minnelli makes a surprise appearance on the song as a guest vocalist.

Taking the role of the Patient's mother, who is engaged in a dialogue with her dying son, Minnelli was asked if she would agree to sing on *The Black Parade* by Rob Cavallo. 'Gerard was kind of joking around,' recalled Ray. 'There's this part in the song Gerard did in a female voice and we weren't happy with it. [Cavallo] just asked, "Who would you want to sing that part?" Gerard said, "I don't know, someone like Liza Minnelli maybe?" A couple of days later we got the word she'd sing on the record.'

'Her publicist explained to her, "There's this young rock band that's a big fan of you, and they would love you to cut this one line off their record, because they need you to do it,"' explained Gerard. 'Then she heard *Revenge*, and she said she was in.'

Sadly, logistical issues made it impossible for the band and Minnelli to actually hook up in the same studio, so the Academy Award-winning actress and singer recorded her part from New York. 'We are big fans of Liza and my grandmother loved her. She was her favourite singer so it was a nod to her,' Gerard told *The Sun*. 'We didn't meet up to record the song but if the opportunity arises to perform it together then we will jump at it.'

Featuring the same acoustic guitar that Billie Joe Armstrong used on Green Day's 1997 hit 'Good Riddance (Time Of Your Life)', 'Sleep' begins portentously with a piano intro overlaid with a vari-speeded vocal sample that recounts 'terrors' and uses the phrase, 'it felt as if someone was gripping my throat.' 'I really love the mood it creates,' declared Frank, 'It's inspired by nerd movies and a haunted house in Hollywood Hills. I love the tape recorder thing that Gerard did – it creeps me out.'

The dynamic, anthemic quality of the track reinforces the valedictory nature of Gerard's lyric. Originally intended as the album's final track, this is the Patient's '*Non, je ne regrette rien*,' his final acceptance of imminent death underpinned by looking back at his life, reaching a resigned conclusion evident in such lines as, "Cos there ain't no way/That I'm coming back again.'

## 'When you do it from the heart, you can do no wrong.' – Bob Bryar

Released in July 2007 as the fourth and final single from *The Black Parade*, 'Teenagers' has its origins in Gerard's nervousness around groups of youths he encountered on his daily subway ride into New York during the album's pre-production. 'The song came directly from commuting when school let out and being so terrified of them,' Gerard told *Revolver* magazine. 'I was like, "Wait a minute – these are the same people who listen to our band. Why am I scared?" And I realised it was because they're scared, too. Teenagers are made to feel like they can only solve their problems with violence. They lash out at each other in a really volatile way.'

Like 'I Don't Love You', 'Teenagers' departs from the core *Black Parade* storyline, this time to explore teenage violence. 'It's a commentary on kids being viewed as meat; by the government and by society. That's how I felt in school, and after 9/11 happened that's how I felt in general. It's very important that this song is here because I always viewed this as about these kids in the parade who had killed themselves, who had made a big mistake.'

Musically, it's easy to appreciate why Reprise selected the song for release as a single. Pounding and infectious, it possesses a sing-along quality reminiscent of the glam-rock and barroom stompers of such early 1970s bands as T.Rex, Slade and the Faces.

The Black Parade's penultimate track, 'Disenchanted', returns the album's focus to the Patient's final moments. Described by Kerrang! as 'a sweeping wall of melancholy', the song again makes effective use of Billie Joe's guitar before exploding into a string-infused stadium rock anthem. Once again, Gerard's lyrics interweave his own experience into the Patient's narrative through lines such as, 'I spent my high school career/Spit on and shoved to agree.'

> 'My parents love the album. They love it so much, and they get it on such a different level.' – Gerard Way

'Famous Last Words' brings the story of the Patient to an unexpectedly upbeat close. Almost the musical equivalent of a literary or cinematic 'MacGuffin', the album's final song sees its protagonist achieving a kind of deliverance. 'The album takes a turning point,' explained Gerard. 'At the very end there's "Famous Last Words", which is very much about redemption.' This upbeat denouement is evident in lyrics such as 'I am not afraid to keep on living / I am not afraid to walk this world alone,' as well as in the soaring guitars and driving rhythm of the arrangement.

The Black Parade also contains a hidden fourteenth track, 'Blood', which pops into existence around 90 seconds after the end of 'Famous Last Words'. A brief, humorous coda to the album, the song features Gerard, accompanied by piano, in full vaudevillian mode for an upbeat ditty on the topic of all things haemoglobular.

The album package was topped off with a booklet that made use of Gerard's artistic prowess, highlighting his vision of the Parade to great effect. Additionally, a limited-run special edition of the album was issued, featuring a faux velvet sleeve and containing a 64-page booklet crammed with Gerard's character designs and conceptual visualisations. 'I think we're very lucky to have Gerard and he's an amazing artist,' affirmed Bob. 'He is very visual with what he does and he'll draw out any ideas that he has. It shows us what he's thinking in his head and it's great to have him do that.'

Speaking in Metal Hammer, Gerard declared himself delighted with the finished product. 'I can't wait to tour and play it live. This is the best and craziest thing that has happened to me and I thank the other four dudes for that. I owe them.'

'We went into this record thinking that we were as tight as we could possibly be – as friends and as family,' Frank told Kerrang! 'We came out of it a hundred times closer.

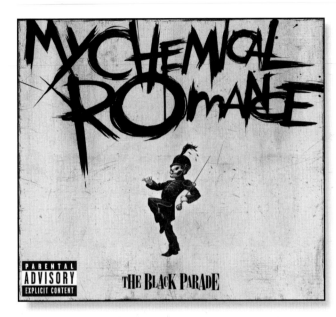

The Black Parade – *a widescreen distillation of My Chem's diversity and vision.*

That was shocking. But I definitely know that this – my family – has our back. That's a great feeling to have when you want to go out and take on the world.'

'What we came out with was something that we are 100 per cent proud of,' Bob asserted. 'It was something that this band has dreamed of doing for a long time. This is what this band is all about and this record completely explains this band at this time.'

In terms of chart success, *The Black Parade* easily surpassed the commercial performance of its predecessor and exceeded record company expectations. Debuting at Number 2 in both the US and UK album charts, within the first week of its release the disc sold slightly under 250,000 copies in America alone. The LP also made the Top Ten in Australia, New Zealand, Ireland, Sweden, Canada, Austria and Greece, as well as cracking the Top Twenty in a number of other territories, such as Italy, Switzerland and Norway. By mid-2007, US sales of *The Black Parade* had comfortably passed the one million mark.

The album received a mostly enthusiastic critical reception; in his four-star *Rolling Stone* review, David Fricke drew comparisons with David Bowie's 1974 album *Diamond Dogs*, describing *The Black Parade* as 'the best mid-seventies record of 2006, a rabid, ingenious paraphrasing of echoes and kitsch from rock's golden age of bombast'. In *Spin*, Andy Greenwald also awarded the disc four stars while asserting, 'it's a savage, heartfelt, at times hilarious goth-mosh emopera'.

*NME*'s Dan Martin gave the album 9/10, identifying how MCR's third album further distanced the band from anything vaguely 'emo'. 'This is crisp, vast and fiercely melodic stadium punk that's barely emo in the slightest,' he wrote. Over at *Kerrang!*,

Tom Bryant turned in an enthusiastic four-K write-up, commenting on the 'fundamental shifts in attitude' that were evident in the musical content and observing how 'beneath the surface is where to look on this album. Underneath the imagery and the concept is where you'll find all sorts – hope, resignation, anger, defiance, self-loathing and a thousand more emotions besides. It'll take a few listens but, when *The Black Parade* reveals its secrets to you, you'll be dazzled by its brilliance.'

However, the pomp and swagger of *The Black Parade* was never likely to be everyone's cup of laudanum. In the *Observer Music Monthly*, Jaimie Hodgson railed against the whole concept of theatricality: 'it reeks of a band with ideas above their station. Worse, it employs a pseudo-theatrical feel, as if they're Meat Loaf's spoilt nephews.' Writing on the *Aversion.com* site, Matt Schild expanded his initial, one-word summation of the LP ('lame') to opine, 'You can't figure out if you just heard the worst prog-rock album ever, the worst off-Broadway soundtrack ever, or the worst Goth-punk album ever.'

'We knew that this record would either get ones or fives. You either get it or you don't,' Gerard told the *Orange County Register*. Speaking to *Metal Hammer* in 2007, the My Chem frontman torpedoed accusations that the album's unique form and content were in any way determined by Reprise. 'The critical reaction was just cynicism. I read something saying, "this is some major label thing and you can tell that the label directs them, yadda yadda yadda." It's like, what label in the world would dress us like that? Have you seen what we look like lately? Who would dress us like that? We had people at the label fucking terrified of the way we looked!'

Realistically, any modern band hoping to pander to the critics would be insane to put together a concept album based upon death, let alone one that incorporated elements of theatricality and pomp-rock – all unfashionable, well-established soft targets for ridicule. The only people that My Chemical Romance were hoping to reach with *The Black Parade* were their fans. 'Our fans are so smart, so special and so unique that I feel this record is a reflection of them,' declared Gerard.

For their part, the MCRmy lapped up the new album. The *Observer* ran a piece by Sarah Boden that rebutted Jaimie Hodgson's scathing review, quoting My Chem fans such as Clare Davis: 'My Chemical Romance's music is about passion, emotions and letting your feelings out. If your writer doesn't feel these emotions, honestly, he shouldn't be reviewing any music – especially passionate rock music.' In the same piece, sixteen-year-old Stacey Martin asserted, 'There are so many people out there, like me, who love MCR and all their hard work. The same people who go to all their gigs and in some cases, owe their lives to MCR's music. *That's* who this album is for! Their devoted and loving fans.'

Fans who were also delighted by the band's return to live action in the wake of *The Black Parade*. After a ten-month hiatus, the group resumed gigging on 25 October with a special album-launch show at the 1400-capacity Webster Hall nightclub and concert venue in New York. The concert heralded a short run of shows during late November that climaxed with an appearance at the KROQ-sponsored Halloween show at the House of Blues in L.A.

November saw MCR travel to Europe for a three-week run of shows that also included a short tour of the UK's larger concert halls. Beginning at the Bournemouth International Centre on 11 November, the five-date tour also took in the Brixton Academy, which led *Evening Standard* critic André Paine to draw comparisons between Gerard and Freddie Mercury, observing that the My Chem frontman 'is one of the most charismatic of the new breed of US rock singers, albeit a slightly earnest one'. Writing in *Kerrang!*, Terry Bezer was unequivocal with his praise: 'With Number 1 singles, critical acclaim and the world's most passionate fans behind them, it's hard to see just what My Chemical Romance can't achieve. On this evening's evidence, the answer is nothing.'

> **'I can't honestly say what makes me sexy . . . I don't feel very sexy.' – Gerard Way**

On 14 November, MCR played Glasgow's Barrowlands. It was a show that was particularly gratifying for Gerard, as it enabled him to hook up with one of his most enduring creative influences, Scottish writer Grant Morrison. Along with Alan Moore and Neil Gaiman, Morrison was at the vanguard of a host of British creators who took the comic book medium into new, literate and often highly surrealistic realms during the late 1980s and 1990s. Responsible for revitalising such half-forgotten DC series as *Animal Man* and *The Doom Patrol*, he also created groundbreaking titles like the William Burroughs/Robert Anton Wilson/Aleister Crowley-inspired *Invisibles* and its thematic sequel, *The Filth*.

Speaking after the show, Morrison praised Gerard's ability to draw positivity from such grim concepts as death, loss, addiction and alienation. 'You gotta embrace that stuff, and absorb it. Steal it back, make it life-affirming again.'

Grant Morrison's unique approach to writing comics would be an influence on *The Umbrella Academy*, Gerard's return to the world of comic books. Speaking to the *NME* in October 2006, the former *Breakfast Monkey* creator explained, 'I draw whenever I get the chance. It's another creative outlet. I need to be able to draw. I just struck a deal with Dark Horse Comics to do my first comic, *The Umbrella Academy*. It's a very bizarre *Doom Patrol*-ish kind of comic.'

Illustrated by Brazilian artist Gabriel Bá, the six-issue mini-series tells the story of Sir Reginald Hargreeves – a 'world renowned scientist and inventor, intrepid adventurer, successful entrepreneur, champion cricketer and closet space alien'. Speaking to the newly relaunched *Comics International* in early 2007, Gerard was quick to acknowledge the influence of Grant Morrison. 'That guy has more ideas in his pinky than most people do in a lifetime, and he doesn't mind tossing all of them into just one issue. His run on *Doom Patrol* and Wes Anderson's *The Royal Tenenbaums* were two of my biggest influences for the series, along with my experience from being in a rock band on the road.'

Back on the road in Europe, My Chem gave a triumphant Milan show which saw Gerard open proceedings with a tongue-in-cheek 'Hello, Vienna!' The quintet then returned to the US for a run of gigs that began on 29 November at Lupo's Heartbreak Hotel in Providence, Rhode Island, and would take them through to mid-December. These shows saw the band appear with such diverse acts as Papa Roach, Taking Back Sunday, Gnarls Barkley and OK Go, and were in many respects a warm-up for the full-scale *Black Parade* tour due to kick off the following year.

> **'It's funny to go from underrated to overrated so quickly. You get so exposed it becomes less cool to be into your band.' – Gerard Way**

For Ray, the complex arrangements that suffused *The Black Parade* presented fresh challenges in transferring them to live performance. 'It was a little difficult for me especially when we first started doing them,' he explained. 'There's a lot of singing for me. On the record Gerard does all his harmonies himself. Live, I have to do them. You have to program your brain to play the guitar parts and sing at the same time. The songs are just a ton of fun to play. The kids' response to the new stuff is even better than the previous two albums.'

The 16 December issue of *Kerrang!* saw My Chemical Romance sweep the boards at the magazine's annual end-of-year poll. Illustrating the polarising effect that My Chem have, the quintet topped the 'Best Band' and 'Worst Band' categories, as well as the polls for the best and worst things about 2006. Similarly, *The Black Parade* was named as both best and worst album of the year, while Gerard was installed as both 'Hero' and 'Villain'

*Gerard Way – from overweight outsider to global rock icon.*

of 2006. Additionally, the silver-haired vocalist topped the 'Sexiest Male' category and made an unexpected fourth-place showing on the 'Sexiest Female' category – from which he was ultimately disqualified, on the grounds of not actually being a woman.

'If we weren't polarising people our lives would be so boring; we wouldn't be affecting anything,' asserted Gerard in response to the poll results. 'If you look at a lot of great bands through rock history they've affected people in both ways: no band that has taken a risk or spoken their minds or that has challenged anything has done it without inspiring love and hate.'

My Chem's year ended on a slightly odd note, when their appearance on the New Year's Eve edition of *Jimmy Kimmel Live* was undermined by the accidental broadcast of rehearsal footage. Once the error was realised, the late-night talk show's production department issued the following statement: 'We apologise for any inconvenience this may have caused the band or their fans. Please tune in on Monday, January 15th when their actual performance will be broadcast – complete with fireworks.'

## 'We were all loners and outcasts in some ways and we still feel like that woven with fame and success.' – Gerard Way

With their 2007 schedule shaping up as another touring endurance marathon, the quintet savoured an extended holiday furlough before travelling to Japan for a short run of shows, moving on to New Zealand and Australia to join the travelling Big Day Out festival with Muse, Tool and Trivium. Unfortunately, before the quintet had even made it as far as the Antipodes, Frank experienced an unpleasantly bloody reaction to the removal of some wisdom teeth that necessitated his return to the US. While he was at home under medication, Drive By guitarist Todd Price filled in for the band's southern hemisphere shows.

These gigs were also notable for the paired-down *Black Parade* stage show. Despite the theatrical nature of the album, it was decided that the emphasis should be upon the band and their music rather than distracting visual elements. 'That helps keep it honest and special and not distract from what we really want to do,' explained Gerard. 'And, frankly, I didn't really want to travel with a bunch of people anymore. We're a really tight family. We should be able to do this with just us.'

Another change was that Gerard had reverted back to his normal ebony hair colour. '[Being blond] served a purpose, 'cos it was like method acting during the record,' he told *Kerrang!*'s Rod Yates. 'Then when the record came out, I still wanted to retain that, but after a while I began to feel less and less like myself in a negative way.'

> 'I don't want to read somebody telling me how awesome I am, just like I don't want to read someone telling me how bad I suck.' – Gerard Way

One enhancement MCR did make to their stage show was the addition of keyboard player James DeWees, who joined the group for the start of the *Black Parade* tour proper, which kicked off with a show at the Verizon Wireless Arena, in Manchester, New Hampshire on 22 February. At his debut show, Gerard introduced James to the New Hampshire crowd as his 'big brother'. Formerly with Kansas City emo outfit the Get Up Kids, DeWees was a close friend of the group and had been ordained as a church minister so he could officiate at the wedding of Mikey and his fiancée, Alicia Simmons – which took place after the band's Las Vegas gig on 7 March 2007. Often the most private member of the band, Mikey made no public statement about his marriage (although his brother and best man subsequently confirmed the groom was 'enjoying it all'.)

For these concerts, the band took the stage as 'the Black Parade', with Gerard making his entrance by way of a hospital bed wheeled onto the stage. Despite the absence of a dance troupe, the band's new stage show was epic in scale. Embellished with huge amounts of pyrotechnics, cannon fire, gunshots and explosive bursts of confetti, the gigs were divided into two halves: the first featuring MCR's wilder, more aggressive, military-clad alter egos, and the second seeing them return as 'themselves' for a run-through of pre-*Black Parade* hits.

My Chem's initial 2007 run of US dates closed on 16 March in Reno, and the band travelled to the UK to begin the European leg of the *Black Parade* tour, commencing four days later with a show at the Plymouth Pavilions. The British shows were notable for the sheer intensity of crowd reaction, with near hysteria holding sway amid mass sing-alongs and thunderous receptions. In his *NME* tour diary, Frank enthused, 'I'm having the time of my life and the kids at these shows are making my dreams come true.' In *Kerrang!* Emma Johnston was equally enthusiastic, giving MCR's 22 March show at Birmingham's huge National Indoor Arena, a five-K thumbs up and declaring, 'Right at this moment, there *are* no other bands.'

After a live national radio broadcast from London's Koko concert hall on 2 April, My Chem headed to mainland Europe for shows in Germany, France, Sweden and

Denmark, before returning to the USA for a string of dates supported by Muse. On 19 April, Gerard announced via the band's official website that, from 5 May, Mikey would be temporarily replaced as bassist by guitar technician Matt Cortez. 'The band has decided to give him and his wife a much needed break from the road to start a life and have a proper honeymoon and do all the things a newlywed couple should do . . . I know this is upsetting news, as it is for us, but we will continue to tour with a temporary replacement until he has situated himself in his new life.'

Asked by *Kerrang!*'s Tom Bryant whether Mikey's leave of absence might also be due to a recurrence of the depression experienced during the recording of *The Black Parade*, Frank was quick to reassure fans. 'No, that's not true. Tell everyone not to be worried about him at all. He's left for a much better thing than that, we should all be very happy for him and should wish him well.'

> 'If I had to work at McDonald's for the rest of my life to play shows and ride in a shitty van on tour? I've done it. I'll do it again.' – Frank Iero

Aside from an outbreak of food poisoning that affected almost the entire touring party, causing a number of cancellations (and leading to death threats against an unfortunate café owner whose establishment was mistakenly identified as the source), My Chem's gigs with Muse were huge, celebratory affairs featuring two bands whose command of the more grandiose elements of modern rock had few contemporary equals.

My Chem's first concert without Mikey was the Bamboozle Festival at the Meadowlands Sports Complex in East Rutherford, New Jersey, where the quintet closed the main stage atop a bill that also included New Found Glory, Paramore and former baggy-trousered chart topper MC Hammer – making what *Kerrang!* described as 'a hilariously bad guest appearance'.

After Bamboozle, MCR played two further dates in Portland, Maine and Worcester, Massachusetts, before travelling north to Canada for a run of eight shows. The band completed the second North American leg of the tour with a gig at the Rose Quarter Memorial Coliseum in Portland, Oregon, took a few short days off and then flew to Tokyo for a show at the Budokan on 29 May.

As the 2007 European festival season got underway, MCR flew in for a series of high-profile headlining appearances. Although the group had become fixtures across many of the major outdoor events, in an interview with *NME*'s Phil Wallis, Gerard confessed that,

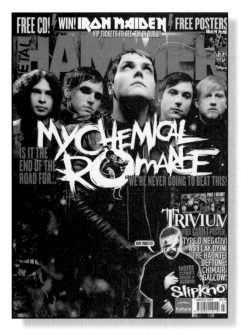

despite enjoying the Big Day Out and even the previous year's Reading show, he was no great fan of festivals. 'I don't like them at all . . . They have a sense of chaos about them. If you look at the riots that happened at Woodstock in 1999, there's always that thing that if you have someone irresponsible onstage, they can cause a real big problem.'

On 8 June, My Chem headlined the annual Download metalfest at Donnington Park racetrack, topping a bill that also included ageing supergroup Velvet Revolver, retro rockers Wolfmother and turgid metal behemoths Megadeth. Download was a three-day event, with nu-metal hangovers Linkin Park headlining the second day and Iron Maiden closing the festival the following night. Gerard was particularly aware of Maiden's metal legacy when asked by *Kerrang!*'s Emma Johnston how he felt about headlining. 'It's a phenomenally huge honour. The festival itself has such a long history. It seems like it's Maiden's festival, because they've had some of their biggest, greatest moments there. So that makes it extra special to me, being a huge Maiden fan.'

> **'We're having the best time of our lives right now. It's like a train that keeps going and going. It's unreal.' – Gerard Way**

'Going out on that stage at Download was great,' enthused Frank after the gig. 'To play a slot that bands like Black Sabbath have played means you have some legendary shoes to fill. All we wanted was to do it justice – to put on the best show that we could.'

Although MCR's set received an enthusiastic reception from the gathered metal multitude, the band drew criticism from the former self-styled 'God of Fuck', Marilyn Manson, who had appeared at Download supporting Linkin Park. With his popularity on the wane, the 38-year-old recent divorcee may have been hoping to drum up some column inches to promote his seventh studio album, *Eat Me, Drink Me*, which had been issued on 5 June to widespread public indifference and poor reviews.

Manson revealed that the track 'Mutilation Is The Sincerest Form Of Flattery' was written with My Chem in mind: 'I'm embarrassed to be me because these people are doing a really sad, pitiful, shallow version of what I've done.' Speaking to *Rock Sound*, Gerard dismissed the ageing shock-rocker's comment as merely that of someone looking to sell product. 'If Elvis Costello said we sucked we would think about it a bit, but usually it is comments from someone with a new record to promote so the remarks ring hollow.'

As My Chemical Romance travelled across Europe on their summer festival schedule, Frank confessed that, despite the warm receptions and good relations among the band, he was missing Mikey. 'I miss the shit out of him,' declared the guitarist. 'I'm so pissed off he isn't here. I want him to come back as soon as humanly possible.'

> 'A part of living your life is to fuck up.' – Frank Iero

While Mikey settled into married life and purchased a puppy, the rest of the group visited Moscow and Venice before returning to England to play one of the first gigs at the recently rebuilt Wembley Stadium. For Gerard, playing in front of 70,000 people at the perpetually chilly hilltop soccer stadium brought back some of the nervousness that he experienced during the band's earliest shows. 'We were such a baby band then and I remember getting up onstage, thinking, "I'm not prepared for this." That's exactly the feeling I had when we walked out at Wembley. I thought, "Oh my . . ."'

Of course, Gerard no longer has any cause to feel nervous. The gig was a huge celebration of his band's unique approach to rock'n'roll. The quintet can now lay claim to being among the biggest rock acts on the planet, and have inspired and delighted fans in dozens of countries. Not that such widespread success carries much weight with Frank. 'Honestly, we're just a punk band from Jersey,' insisted the guitarist. 'If this all ends tomorrow then we'll still be a punk band from Jersey. If we end up back in basements playing "I'm Not Okay" to 50 kids, then I'm still psyched. That's all I ever wanted anyway.'

'What we wanted has never changed,' agreed Gerard. 'We've exceeded our goals, so anything that's happened musically since last year has been a nice little bonus. I think that you'll find that anyone in this band would be happy playing to a room of 100 kids.'

My Chemical Romance's turbo-charged rise to global stardom is a victory for the

*The 2007 Projekt Revolution tour saw Frank sporting a new look.*

underdog, the outsider, the loner kid who gets picked on for being different. 'I don't think anything could ever take that underdog-ness away, because we're still in this big gene pool, and we're the one chromosome that doesn't fit,' Gerard told Neala Johnston of Australian newspaper the *Herald Sun*. 'If you look at videos being played, you have our video up against hip hop, pop, boy bands, girl bands, divas . . . and then there's this little rock band. We're never gonna fit in.'

**'All our dreams have come true so far. Anything from here on is just going to be a blessing.' – Frank Iero**

Despite the wealth and status that being the frontman of a massively successful global rock phenomenon affords, it is still the affect that the group has on ordinary people that means the most to Gerard. 'We're really happy that all of our ethics, our philosophy, and creativity is translating well,' he told the *MusicPix* website. 'We actually kind of expected to be swept under the rug because we've seen many of our friends with the same intentions get swept under the rug. So we feel really lucky and really blessed to have it work worldwide.'

Reflecting on the band's rise, Frank intimated that he hoped that the way in which MCR sprung from a small regional scene to worldwide recognition in five short years would be repeated by others. 'I hope the world isn't the same place after this band, as it was before this band,' he explained to *Metal Edge* magazine. 'I'd like to see a change in music, in the way things are done – real bands coming back, kids setting up and having something to say. When kids can put a band together, write a song in their basement and put that on the internet and change things . . . then that's a really scary time for music. And that's amazing.'

'For us, it's never been about a job,' declared Frank. 'If we can change people's lives with our passion, with something we love, that's the ultimate gift. And every day with this band is a gift.'

*Thank you and goodnight – despite My Chem's massive success,*
*Gerard has always asserted that the band owe everything to their fans.*

# SELECTED DISCOGRAPHY

## SINGLES

Honey, This Mirror Isn't Big Enough For The Two Of Us / This Is The Best Day Ever
Eyeball Records, 2002
US

Headfirst For Halos / Our Lady Of Sorrows
Warner/Reprise, 2004
US

Thank You For The Venom / Jack The Ripper (live)
Warner/Reprise, 2004
Europe

I'm Not Okay (I Promise) / Bury Me In Black (demo) / You Know What They Do To Guys Like Us In Prison (live)
Warner/Reprise, 2005
US/Europe

Helena / I'm Not Okay (I Promise) (live)
Warner/Reprise, 2005
US/Europe

The Ghost Of You / Helena (live)
Warner/Reprise, 2005
US/Europe

Welcome To The Black Parade / Heaven Help Us
Warner/Reprise, 2006
US/Europe

Famous Last Words / My Way Home Is Through You
Warner/Reprise, 2007
US/Europe

I Don't Love You / Cancer (live)
Warner/Reprise, 2007
US/Europe

Teenagers / Dead! (live)
Warner/Reprise, 2007
US/Europe

## ALBUMS

*I Brought You My Bullets, You Brought Me Your Love*
Romance / Honey, This Mirror Isn't Big Enough For The Two Of Us / Vampires Will Never Hurt You / Drowning Lessons / Our Lady Of Sorrows / Headfirst For Halos / Skylines And Turnstiles / Early Sunsets Over Monroeville / This Is The Best Day Ever / Cubicles / Demolition Lovers
Eyeball Records, 2002
US

*Three Cheers For Sweet Revenge*
Helena / Give 'Em Hell, Kid / To The End / You Know What They Do To Guys Like Us In Prison / I'm Not Okay (I Promise) / The Ghost Of You / The Jetset Life Is Gonna Kill You / Interlude / Thank You For The Venom / Hang 'Em High / It's Not A Statement, It's A Deathwish / Cemetery Drive / I Never Told You What I Do For A Living
Warner/Reprise, 2004
US/Europe

*The Black Parade*
The End / Dead! / This Is How I Disappear / The Sharpest Lives / Welcome To The Black Parade / I Don't Love You / House Of Wolves / Cancer / Mama / Sleep / Teenagers / Disenchanted / Famous Last Words / Blood
Warner/Reprise, 2006
US/Europe

## LIVE ALBUM

*Life On The Murder Scene*
Thank You For The Venom / Cemetery Drive / Give 'Em Hell, Kid / Headfirst For Halos / Helena / You Know What They Do To Guys Like Us In Prison / The Ghost Of You / I'm Not Okay (I Promise) / I Never Told You What I Do For A Living (demo) / Bury Me In Black (demo) / Desert Song (previously unreleased)
Warner/Reprise, 2005
US/Europe

# ACKNOWLEDGEMENTS

A number of people have provided invaluable assistance, without which this book would have proven impossible to write. Chief among these are Abbey Needs and Anna Jones. Many thanks also to the following photographers: Steve Brown/Retna for the cover photograph; Frank White (Pages 42, 59, 67, 79, 80, 85, 105, 109, 110,115, 123, 127, 137, 139,140, 147, 153, 154); Redferns/NAKI; Retna/Nick Stevens; Retna/Anthony Saint James; Retna/David Atlas; Getty/ Eddie Malluk; Retna/John McMurtle; Getty/Scott Gries; Redferns/Christina Radish; Redferns/Hayley Madden; Retna/Kevin Estrada; Retna/Daragh McDonach; Getty/ James Sharrock; Getty/Wireimage/John Shearer; Retna/Dave Williams; Getty/Wireimage/Bill McCay. The following journalists, articles, publications and internet publications proved invaluable in producing this book, and many of which will provide excellent sources for all MCR fans. The author would like to express his thanks for their work: *Alternative Press*, 10/05 feature: Leslie Simon; *Alternative Press*, 01/06 feature: Jason Pettigrew; *Alternative Press*, 01/07 feature: Jason Pettigrew; *AMP*, 06/04 feature: Jeff Schechter; *Billboard*, 21/04/05 tour feature: John Benson; *Billboard*, 28/02/07 live review: Gary Graff; *Billboard*, 09/03/07 interview: Gary Graff; *Blender*, 08/04 interview: Nick Duerden; *Blender*, 08/04 album review: Andy Greenwald; *Blender*, 04/05 feature: Dorian Lynksey; *Blender*, 12/06 tour feature: Andy Greenwald; *Brandenton Herald*, 19/02/07 interview: Brian McCollum; *Chartattack.com*, 11/04 interview: Pete Richards; *Chicago Sun Times*, 25/02/07 interview: Jim de Rogatis; *Cincinnati City Beat*, 22/03/04 interview: Alan Sculley; *Comic Book Resources*, 23/02/07 news item: Andy Khouri; *Comics International*, 04/07 news item: Mike Conroy; *Concertlivewire.com*, 28/06/05 interview: Phil Bonyata & Karen Bondowski; *Courier Mail*, 14/10/06 tour feature: James Wigney; *Crush Media*, 18/06/04 interview: Jason Schleweis & Rob Todd; *Daily Mail*, 16/08/06 article: Sarah Sands; *Daily Trojan*, 03/06/07 interview: Kari Kramer; *Deseret Morning News*, 02/03/07 article: Amanda Pierce; *Designer Magazine*, 03/05 interview: Alex McCann; *Disorder*, 10/06 feature: Taylor Glasby; *Doom Patrol*, #19-63 DC Comics 1988-93: Grant Morrison; *Dose.ca*, 17/10/06 news item: Heather Adler; *Dose.ca*, 24/10/06 news item: Heather Adler; *Dose.ca*, 13/11/06 feature: Christne Clarke; *Drownedinsound.com*, 25/08/06 interview: Mike Diver; *Entertainment Weekly*, 08/12/06 interview: Whitney Pastorek; *Epiphone News*, 31/08/04 interview: Don Mitchell; *Evening Standard*, 13/11/06 live review: André Paine; *Fasterlouder.com*, 03/11/06 music feature: kbro; *Guardian*, 09/04/04 album review: Caroline Sullivan; *Guardian*, 07/02/05 live review: Betty Clarke; *Guardian*, 20/10/06 album review: Betty Clarke; *Guardian*, 27/10/06 article: Alexis Petridis; *Guardian*, 14/11/2006 live review: Caroline Sullivan; *Guardian Unlimited*, 24/01/07 news feature: Paul MacInnes; *Herald Sun*, 28/12/06 interview: Neala Johnson; *The Invisibles*, #1-25 DC Comics 1994-96: Grant Morrison; *The Independent*, 26/08/05 interview: Elisa Bray; *Iowa State Daily*, 02/05/05 interview: Darin Longman; *Kerrang!*, 28/10/04 album review: Tom Bryant; *Kerrang!*, 17/02/07 live review: Rod Yates; *Kerrang!*, 17/03/07 interview: Emma Johnston; *Kerrang!*, 07/04/07 live review: Emma Johnston; *Kerrang!*, 05/05/07 feature: Tom Bryant; *Kerrang!*, 26/05/07 live review: Nichola Browne; *Kerrang!*, 09/06/07 interview: Emma Johnston, Dan Slessor; *Kerrang!*, 30/06/07 tour diary: Tom Bryant; *LA Times*, 12/03/07 live review: Richard Cromelin; *Livedaily.com*, 08/02/07 interview: Christina Fuoco; *Livedaily.com*, 12/03/07 live review: Christina Fuoco-Karasinski; *Modern Drummer*, 04/07 interview: Waleed Rashidi; *MTV.com*, 23/06/04 album feature: Jon Wiederhorn; *MTV.com*, 09/11/04 news feature: James Montgomery/Chris Ward; *MTV.com*, 17/11/04 news feature: James Montgomery; *MTV.com*, 07/01/05 news feature: James Montgomery/Corey Moss; *MTV.com*, 28/02/05 interview: James Montgomery; *MTV.com*, 15/03/05 news feature: James Montgomery; *MTV.com*, 25/05/05 news feature: James Montgomery; *MTV.com*, 30/05/05 interview feature: James Montgomery/Corey Moss; *MTV.com*, 15/08/05 news feature: James Montgomery; *MTV.com*, 30/08/05 news feature: James Montgomery; *MTV.com*, 27/09/05 news feature: Chris Harris; *MTV.com*, 05/11/06 news feature: Gil Kaufman; *MTV.com*, 14/03/06 news feature: James Montgomery; *MTV.com*, 10/08/06 news feature: James Montgomery; *MTV.com*, 23/02/07 news feature: John Norris; *Musicpix.net*, 05/05/05 tour interview: Gwyn Tyme; *My*

*Chemical Romance* by Mona Gale, Omnibus Press, 2006; *My Chemical Romance: Something Incredible This Way Comes* by Paul Stenning, Independent Music Press, 2006; *New York Times*, 14/08/05 article: Tammy La Gorce; *New York Times*, 26/10/06 article: Kelefa Sanneh; *New York Times*, 26/02/07 live review: Kelefa Sanneh; *New Zealand Herald*, 22/12/06 interview: Laura McQuillan; *NME*, 14/10/06 album review: Dan Martin; *NME*, 11/11/06 feature: Phil Wallis; *NME*, 24/03/07 live review: Laura Ferreiro; *NME*, 07/04/07 tour diary: Barry Nicolson; *NME*, 26/05/07 interview: Phil Wallis; *Observer*, 10/12/06 article: Sarah Boden; *Observer Music Monthly*, 15/10/06 album review: Jaimie Hodgson; *Orange County Register*, 09/03/07 tour feature: Ben Wener; *Punkbands.com*, 07/02/07 interview: Mike Passaretti; *The Punk Site*, 20/10/04 interview: Gary Hampton; *Rip It Up*, 12/06 interview: Scott McLennan; *Rip It Up*, 01/07 interview: Scott McLennan; *Rocky Mountain News*, 02/03/07 interview: Mark Brown; *Rolling Stone*, 07/05 interview: Steve Baltin; *Rolling Stone*, 09/06 live review: Patrick Berkery; *Rolling Stone*, 11/06 interview: Austin Scaggs; *Rolling Stone*, 07/05 feature: Jenny Eliscu; *Rolling Stone*, 01/07 album review: David Fricke; *Seattle Post-Intelligencer*, 09/07/04 interview: Gene Stout; *Spin*, 05/05 feature: Andy Greenwald; *Spin*, 02/06 interview: Kyle Anderson; *Spin*, 11/06 album review: Andy Greenwald; *Straight.com*, 02/09/04 feature: Mike Usinger; *Suicide Girls*, 09/08/04 interview: Daniel Robert Epstein; *The Sun*, 20/10/06 album feature: Jacqui Swift; *The Sun*, 23/10/06 news feature: Harry McAdam; *Times*, 14/11/06 live review: Lisa Verrico; *VH1.com*, 09/11/05 news feature: James Montgomery; *VH1.com*, 20/10/06 news feature: James Montgomery.

There are a host of My Chem-related websites, many of which contain a wealth of band-related information. The most prominent of these are:
www.mychemicalromance.com
www.imnotokay.net
www.myitalianchemicalromance.com
www.myspace.com/mychemicalromance
www.skeletoncrewonline.com
www.theimmortalityproject.com

There are also a number of excellent, more general websites, which regularly run news items, interviews and features on MCR. Those that proved particularly useful in researching this book include:
www.floridaentertainmentscene.com
www.lifeinabungalo.com
www.metalunderground.com
www.nme.com
www.punknews/org
www.roarezine.com
www.rockdetector.com
www.troublebunchmusic.com
www.angelfire.com/geek/nca/mychemicalromance.html

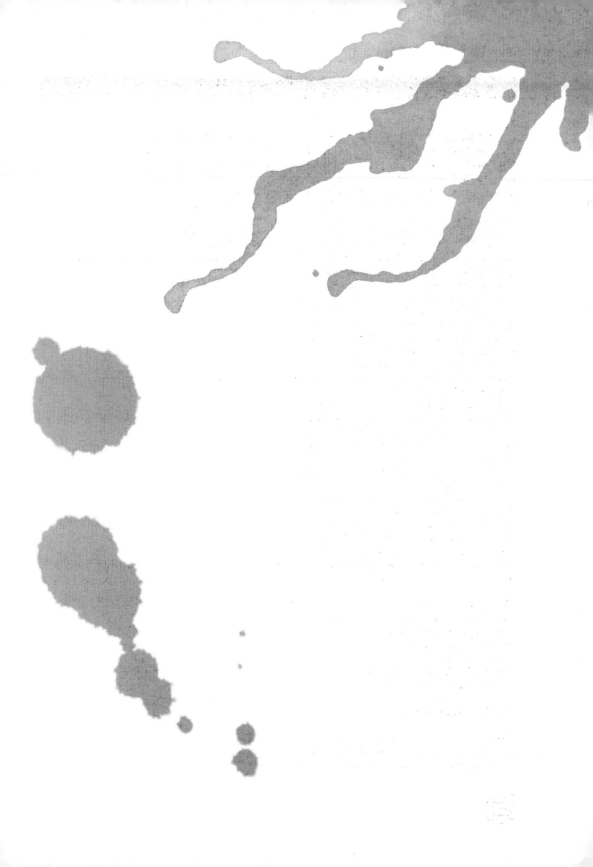